~~~ The Man Who Rode Sharks

	DATE DUE		

William R. Royal
with ROBERT F. BURGESS

The Man Who Rode Sharks

AN AUTHORS GUILD BACKINPRINT.COM EDITION

The Man Who Rode Sharks
All Rights Reserved © 1978, 2000 by William R. Royal
and Robert F. Burgess

AN AUTHORS GUILD BACKINPRINT.COM EDITION

Published by iUniverse.com, Inc.

For information address:
iUniverse.com, Inc.
620 North 48th Street, Suite 201
Lincoln, NE 68504-3467
www.iuniverse.com

Originally published by Dodd, Mean & Company

ISBN: 0-595-00389-3

Printed in the United States of America

FOR GENIE, WHO BELIEVED IN ME

contents

foreword

THIS BOOK TELLS the story of an extraordinary man to whom scientists owe a great debt.

We all know about the scientist whose discovery is the result of meticulous experimentation, painstaking observations through a microscope, or the careful planning of an expedition. But leads into scientific studies sometimes come from a nonscientist who stumbles onto an unusual find and realizes its importance. When such a lead is eventually worked on by teams of specialists, their names are on the resulting publications; their doctoral degrees and professorships give their reports instant credibility and authenticity; it is their work that is held in respect and awe. And the person who made the initial find and brought it to the attention of science is often forgotten.

Colonel William Royal is the key man behind the most exciting archaeological find in Florida. A diver of extraordinary ability, he was the first to explore the deepest sinkholes in Florida and to realize the significance of stalactites he found in underwater caves and evidence he found in thick layers of sediment, all pointing to the existence of Ice Age man living there when the sea level was lower. His reports to scientists sounded incredible. He was labeled a fake and was ridiculed by professionals, who would not or could not check out his unusual evidence, especially when he uncovered an intact, ancient skeleton with a naturally preserved brain inside the skull. Ultimately this proved to be the oldest human brain known, but it took years of Bill Royal's effort before he received the support of Dr. Tilly Edinger, a brain specialist at Harvard, and Dr. Kenneth P. Oakley, an anthropologist at the British Museum. Then, finally, the professionals admitted some belief in Bill's remarkable finds.

Bill Royal has unselfishly devoted decades of his life to helping scientists for little or no pay while pursuing his own insatiable curiosity about the unusual and unknown, especially in the underwater world. He is a gentle, kind and loving man whose patience with adversaries has been truly remarkable. Years of frustration and ridicule from scientists (including those he tried to help) have not embittered him. He understood that his finds and theories of Ice Age man in Florida were hard for anyone to believe at the time. Instead of being angry at not being recognized, he was pleased when his findings were confirmed, even though others received the credit. To him, the "find" was more important than the credit. His way of life is his reward.

I first met Bill in 1958 and have made some of my most interesting, exciting and dangerous dives with him. His coolness in a crisis is most impressive. Once when leading two of us into a deep underwater cave, his regulator jammed and suddenly cut off his air supply. Without letting us know of his problem, he took each of us firmly by the hand, guided us out of the cave, then slowly led us up the seventy-foot distance to the surface.

Bill usually dives alone (something you and I should never do) because it is difficult for him to find a diving buddy, even half his age, who can keep up with him. His precarious pursuits into areas of unknown conditions and uncertain developments threaten danger for most divers who lack his sense of direction in darkness, his calm, cool and collected manner under conditions provoking panic.

Since I first met Bill, I've marveled at his ability to handle sharks and his fearlessness regarding hazardous animals and conditions at sea when we worked together on various scientific projects. I've also marveled at his sense of humor, his love of hard work and his endless energy. Once at sea, after an exhausting and long dive, Bill, the senior member of our expedition who had dived the longest and worked the hardest, amused us with his imitation of a sea lion, barking and leaping in and out of the water and onto the boat with the grace and tireless energy of a child at play, while the rest of us sprawled exhausted on the deck watching his antics. On overnight boat trips he could work with shifts of scientists all day and through half the night, yet be up first the next morning to make coffee for us all.

Bill Royal is a rare and wonderful man. I feel privileged to have been a tiny part in his unique and true adventure story.

EUGENIE CLARK
Professor of Zoology
University of Maryland

PART ONE

The Sharks

1

~~~~~~~~~~~~~ *first encounter*

June 1953, Johnston Island in the South Pacific
I WAS SPEARFISHING alone a hundred yards from the boat
when a tiger shark with pectoral fins so big he looked like
a heavy bomber approached and started circling me. He
was in no hurry. His movements were slow and deliber-
ate. His markings were those of a young adult about
twelve feet long.

As he circled, his eye stayed fixed on me. Suddenly my
rubberband arbalete speargun felt awfully flimsy. Pivot-
ing with the weapon pointed at the shark, I wondered

what he had in mind. If it was what I suspected, I had to act soon.

His actions convinced me. That big mottled gray body gradually kept getting closer until it blotted out a large chunk of scenery. He was about five feet from the end of my arbalete when I fired.

As the shaft slammed into him just behind his pectoral fin, the shark bolted. When he hit the end of my 25-foot, 2,000-pound-test steel spear cable, the jolt almost tore off my mask. He plowed me through the water just long enough for the shaft to tear loose from his side.

I reloaded fast. The shark turned and came back, jaws agape and a decidedly unfriendly look in his eye. I fired. The steel shaft pierced his flank at an angle. Shallow penetration. When it tore out I thought surely the shark would go off and leave me alone. But he didn't. Back he came.

This time I hit him in a softer spot. The spear sank deeper, but again as the shark swerved away the harpoon jerked free. I watched him glide off into the blue, then curve around. I thought, "My God, is he going to make *another* pass at me?"

I fumbled to reload, all thumbs now, spear, cable, rubbers, everything getting in the way. I had no hope of killing something that size. But I also knew there was no chance of getting back to the boat. The minute I turned my back to swim, he would have me. Too, I knew that if just once I didn't get that shaft back into the gun and the rubbers stretched in time it amounted to the same thing.

The shark barreled into range. I held off until he was a scant three feet away. Then the arbalete lurched in my hand, the shaft leaped forward and I was amazed to see the slender steel rod pass entirely through the shark's midsection!

He started circling with the spear dangling from his side, then changed his mind and cut back toward me. There I was, pointing an empty speargun at him!

We collided head-on, his snout meeting the muzzle of my arbalete as hard as I could jab it. He side-slammed me, made an abrupt about-face and tore off, taking everything including my empty arbalete with him. If he changed his mind this time and came back, all he would find waiting for him would be shark bait.

I stared into the blue haze for a moment, hardly daring to breathe. To my relief he did not reappear. He had left for good.

As I swam back to the boat I was acutely aware that something more than chance had spared my life again. Call it whatever you like, but I knew there had been too many times when the outcome could have been—and should have been—different. My whole life has been that way.

I encountered my first shark in 1931. Meeting them in their own element with today's powerful bang-sticks and spearguns is one thing, but lassoing a big shark and hanging in there with him is something else. If you have any sense you don't do it for fun. As most people know, sharks are armed literally from head to tail with teeth, including the dermal denticles of their hide, and they know how to use them. Trying to rope or ride one of these creatures can bring on quick disaster.

Sometimes, however, there is a valid reason for this close encounter between man and shark. Sometimes it is even a necessity. If you consider hunger enough of a reason then you might say I first got into sharks strictly from necessity. But actually it was feet first and full of Midwestern innocence. Or ignorance, if you will. Let me explain.

As a youngster growing up in Michigan in the early 1900s sharks were the furthest thing from my mind. In those days all Midwestern kids knew about sharks was what they read in adventure stories. When you read that "a triangular black fin sliced ominously through the water," you knew immediately that someone was about to be deprived of life or limb. And since sharks and oceans go together, Midwestern kids were about as anxious to get into an ocean as they were to get into their Saturday-night baths. I was a married young man with a family before I ever changed my mind on that subject. And then it took the hunger of the Depression years and a trip to Florida to do it.

In 1931 we were well into what everyone was calling the Great Depression. It had changed the world for me and millions of others. Finding no work in Michigan, I thought perhaps I could find something in Florida. At least it would be sunny and warm there. My father had died the previous spring, so that September I packed my mother, my wife and our infant son, Ivan, into my Essex coupe and headed for Florida. We got as far as the Worthington Hotel in Venice, a small town just south of Sarasota, when we finally were stopped by a hurricane. There was no advance warning about hurricanes in those days; if you got caught in them, you simply tried not to get blown away. With winds up to seventy miles an hour and a raging rainstorm, we took refuge in the hotel, thinking it was as safe a place as any in a storm. I remember us standing forlornly in the middle of our second-story room getting sprayed by rain blowing through the crack in the window sash, and my mother saying, "So *this* is sunny Florida?"

After a few days the weather cleared up and I started looking for work. I went to every business in Sarasota and all the surrounding towns. Eventually I reached the Manatee Crate Mill just east of Bradenton and finally found a job. Eight dollars a week! Unbelievable! I was overjoyed. The job was seasonal, lasting only until the fruit was all packed and shipped for the year. But I was grateful for the work and spent that winter and spring making crates for the fruit shippers.

On eight dollars a week we couldn't afford much recreation, but once a week we would go to Bradenton Beach, about ten miles away, and spend the day swimming and sunning. On the way to the beach we crossed the Cortez Bridge connecting the mainland to Anna Maria Island. The wood bridge was almost half a mile long and was lined with fishermen. From the bridge I could see schools of brilliantly colored fish flashing in the clear bay water—thousands of mullet, huge snook, and drum. At first it was fun to watch them and think about how good it would be to catch a fish dinner to supplement our meager resources. Then I began thinking seriously about trying my luck at fishing.

Nobody fished for fun in those days; they were dead serious about it. Few people could afford fishing tackle so almost everyone used long handlines tied off on the railings. When you hooked a fish you brought him in hand-over-hand, praying that if he was a big one he wouldn't do too much flopping on the way up and break the line. It was quite an art, knowing when a fish was played out enough to bring him up. Too soon and you risked losing him to a broken line. Waiting too long, you risked losing him around a piling. Either way it was a slow process. Too many big fish were lost simply because we lacked adequate means to hold onto them. And these were fish big enough to feed a family of four for several days. This fact started me thinking about a better way to fish, a method that would enable me to hold onto some of those large fish.

I decided to try a harpoon, something I could hurl from above and recover by a rope tied to the shaft. I made one with a long wooden shaft and a barbed trident a welder friend fashioned for me. By trial and error I learned how to throw it accurately enough to start hitting the fish I was after. Gradually I began getting some of the larger fish that lived under the Cortez Bridge, and after modifying the harpoon with weights near its business end, I successfully harpooned large snook weighing over twenty-five pounds apiece, often five or six a day. The local fish market bought the surplus, and the proceeds added a little variety to our diet of fish and citrus fruit.

When my job at the Manatee Crate Mill slowed down to part-time, my family became more dependent than ever on the fish I could harpoon from the Cortez Bridge. Since the bridge was not too high above water it made harpooning relatively easy. But I was constantly trying to land bigger fish. And there was just so much that I could do with my wood-shafted harpoon. So I made another. This time the shaft was a length of half-inch galvanized pipe with the trident head welded on. Drilling a hole in the end of the pipe, I tied on a twenty-five-foot piece of manila rope. This harpoon worked well, and I patrolled the bridge almost every day.

The channel was fifteen to eighteen feet deep. On a clear day you could see almost to the bottom. Big jewfish often swam around pilings where they fed on smaller fish. On several occasions I harpooned the big fish, but they were too heavy to hold and always tore loose. Just one of those fish would have fed us for a week, so I was determined to keep after them until I succeeded in landing one.

Finally I did. I harpooned a jewfish about four feet long that weighed around eighty pounds, but to get him I had to jump in the water with him. Although I was still getting plenty of sheepshead, redfish and snook by hauling them up the side of the bridge impaled on my harpoon, I never minded jumping into the water to fight down something larger, usually a jewfish. Sometimes I would swim them ashore, but usually I would subdue the fish, tie one end of my harpoon rope through their mouth and gill covers, hand my harpoon to someone on the bridge, then climb up through the creosoted crossbraces and haul my catch up onto the bridge behind me. Sometimes I transferred him to a trailing rope stringer. But usually I only did this if I had a full day's harpooning ahead of me and no way to keep the fish from spoiling in the sun on the bridge. Like most of the bridge fishermen I was reluctant to keep my catch on a stringer because it sometimes trolled up a shark. Some anglers lost an entire day's catch that way. Usually, however, the fishermen kept a lookout for the long undulating shadow that meant there was a marauding shark about, and as soon as the shout "Shark!" went up, everyone got their catch out of the water until the predator left.

It was just such an occasion that involved me with my first big shark. I had become acquainted with a man named McKelvy, a New York insurance-company executive who had suffered reverses in the Depression. McKelvy was then working for a local newspaper. His twelve-year-old nephew, Johnny, was my constant companion when I came to the bridge to harpoon fish. Johnny liked watching me harpoon, and he always stood by ready to give me a helping hand if I needed it.

On this particular afternoon the two of us were walking the bridge watching for fish shadows around the pilings when someone shouted, "Hey! There's a big shark under the bridge!"

Everyone got their stringers of fish out of the water, tied off their handlines and hurried down the bridge to see. Johnny and I grabbed the harpoon and ran after them. An excited crowd was bunched at the railing. Looking down I saw the black shape close to the surface of the pilings. It was a lemon shark at least seven feet long. I lifted the harpoon overhead with both hands and hurled it down.

It struck the shark just behind its head. All hell broke loose. The water exploded. I flipped a turn of rope over the rail just as the manila strummed taut. The shark thrashed up a storm beneath us. It charged back and forth trying to get loose. The crowd yelled so loud I hardly heard Johnny shout, "Quick, Bill! The harpoon's pulling free!"

I loosed the rope from the railing and the shark almost yanked my arms out of their sockets. His whole body flexed so violently the water boiled around him. This tug-of-war couldn't last long.

It was the biggest fish I had ever harpooned. I didn't think of it as a shark, just one really big fish that would be food for the family or money at the fish market. But it was going to get away if I couldn't get the noose around its tail. I reacted just like it was a big jewfish about to escape—I jumped off the bridge into the water with him.

The shark was too upset to think about attacking me. As soon as he felt slack in the rope he took off, only he went the wrong way between a pair of pilings. I snubbed him off and he started thrashing again. Quickly I worked my way closer, keeping well behind him. Finally I got close enough to grab his tail and try to get the rope around it.

The shark was immediately unhappy about this. His head swung like a battering ram while I hung onto the lashing tail section for dear life. He slammed me against the wood pilings so hard they felt like concrete. Each time I painfully caromed off those unyielding posts, they seemed to grab at me. Why they did made no impression then. It was only later when I saw my shredded clothes and noticed that half of me was dripping a diluted shade of red that I realized clusters of barnacles had been slicing neat hash marks in my hide.

From catching small sharks on the fishing line I knew they were flexible enough to bend back and almost, but not quite, reach whatever held them just ahead of their tail fin. So, if I wanted to stay healthy I had to hold tight to that tail and keep my body straight back from it. Thank God I had a young man's lung capacity, because in the process I spent more time underwater than on the surface. Every time my head popped out of water I heard the crowd on the bridge going wild. Nobody had ever seen a hand-to-fish fight between a man and a shark before, so there was great excitement. Since most of the spectators probably thought I was a goner, I wouldn't have been the least surprised if there wasn't some fast wagering on the side of the shark.

Myself, I didn't know quite what was going to happen, only that I had a shark by the tail and I couldn't very well let go. In all the thrashing the harpoon pulled loose. The only thing still holding the shark was me. And there was more rope tangled around me than there was around the shark.

Finally, thankfully, I felt his efforts weakening. He was wearing down, but so was I. At least now I was able to fumble with the rope. I pushed a length of it through my spliced hand loop and somehow managed to slip it over the shark's caudal fin. One slashing swipe of his tail and it was tight.

I let go of him, slid my hands along the manila until I felt the cold hard metal shaft of the harpoon, then hung on. Thinking he was free, the shark wobbled off toward the bottom. When he hit the end of the rope and found he couldn't go any farther, he turned and headed back toward me.

There was no mistaking his intentions. Jaws open and mayhem probably on his mind, he lunged for me. I butted him away with the harpoon. He slid past, turned and came back. Again I fended him off. Finally he went to the end of the rope and started some serious bulldogging.

Feeling him weaken once more, I pulled him toward me tail-first. He seemed to have lost his fight, or was he playing possum? I had no intention of testing him. Keeping his tail toward me, I passed the harpoon up to eager hands on the bridge and yelled, "Haul him up!"

While I clung to a piling, the twisting, thrashing, yellowish-brown body slowly rose tail-first from the water, glistening and heavy as it inched past me. Suddenly the shark's head was level with mine and we looked at each other eye-to-eye. As long as I live I will never forget the look in that glaring yellow eye with its almond-shaped black pupil and twitching nictitating membrane. The next instant he made a last head-swinging lunge for me. As his jaws thudded shut on empty air, a shiver shot down my spine. For the first time I realized what kind of animal I had so carelessly jumped into the water with. This was no ordinary fish, it was a streamlined engine of destruction, one whose family members I would eventually admire and respect. But at the moment all I thought was what a feast he was going to make, thankful things weren't the other way around.

On the bridge where he gnashed his teeth and thrashed around in a fine frenzy for the crowd, my catch soon attracted those on the beach as well. Most people came to see what all the yelling and screaming was about.

I brought my car over and willing hands helped load the shark into the trunk—at least most of him got in. Then, feeling like celebrities, Johnny McKelvy, myself and the family drove off to a ragged round of cheers.

Driving home we must have presented an interesting spectacle to those who noticed the better part of a shark's rear end hanging down over the bumper of our Essex coupe.

Johnny McKelvy's uncle photographed the shark and

wrote an article about it for the Bradenton newspaper. The story was picked up by the Associated Press and before long people across the country were reading about the crazy man who fought a shark bare-handed.

As a reward for my efforts we enjoyed shark steaks for days and days and days. Moreover, the incident made me such a hero at the Manatee Crate Mill that I was almost the last man to be laid off. How fleeting is fame.

2

the halstead project

WHEN WE FLEW over Johnston Island and I saw it for the first time, I couldn't believe my luck in being stationed there for a year or more. Johnston is a dot in the Pacific 760 miles southwest of Honolulu, a speck of land three fifths of a mile long, 600 feet wide and 12 to 14 feet high at the highest part of the island. From the air I saw little vegetation, mostly small shrubs and bunch grass. Everything was bisected by runways and taxiways of the Johnston Island U.S. Air Force Base, where I had been assigned as civil engineer.

The island was no Bali Hai by any means. In fact it seemed the most unromantic island in the entire Pacific. Then I took a closer look at the setting surrounding this flawed gem and caught my breath. I saw miles of shallow-water flats, ravines, pockets, walls of undulating coral reefs, acres of underwater gardens—the entire scene hitting every hue in the blue-green spectrum so vividly that the sea around the island seemed to glow. This unique effect was caused by light reflecting off the white-sand bottom through varying depths of water over the shallow eight-mile-long bank that supports Johnston Island and a much smaller islet a mile to the northeast called Sand Island. Part of this bank is rimmed by an irregular arrow-shaped coral reef flanking the islands to the northwest for six miles before breaking up into an extensive area of patch reefs to the north. Southeast of the island the bank is a four- to five-mile-long coral shoal sloping gradually down to the 100-fathom curve. A ship channel dredged through this shoal area forms a lagoon accessible to large vessels.

As we swung in for our approach to the island I was especially impressed with the silhouettes of big sharks and manta rays dotting the watery landscape below. Some of the rays appeared to be sixteen or eighteen feet across. And there were schools of them!

The population of Johnston Island averaged around 1,000, about two thirds military and one third civilian. Except for a few officers' wives, most of the civilians were Polynesians from other Pacific islands.

The earliest mention of the atoll is in the records of the American ship *Sally*, which ran aground there in 1796. The next visit was in 1807 by H.R.M.S. *Cornelius*. The larger of the two coral atolls was named for her skipper, Charles J. Johnston. The island was claimed for the United States on March 19, 1858, by the captain of the ship *Palestine.* This newly acquired piece of American property, in one of the driest areas of the Pacific, remained uninhabited until 1909, when it was leased from the Territory of Hawaii by a private guano company. The highest spot on the island, the forty-foot "Summit Peak" at the eastern end, is apparently part of a guano deposit that was partially removed. After that venture failed, the island was made a bird reservation in 1926. In 1934 the atoll was placed under the jurisdiction of the U.S. Navy, but it was late 1939 before military personnel inhabited the island.

Whether or not conditions were similar for early inhabitants, by 1953 the main problem on the island was boredom. The airstrip was a refueling depot for transpacific flights, but since the Korean conflict had simmered down, things had become so quiet we felt forgotten in the backwaters of the war.

Outside of routine duties the personnel had little to do. With over six hundred men on the island and only fifty women, frequent passes had to be issued for "rest and rehabilitation" in Honolulu to keep up morale.

Off-duty hours on Johnston were usually spent in one of three clubs—one for officers, one for NCOs and one for enlisted men. At least half of the high-ranking civilians and many of the military were fast becoming alcoholics in their spare time just to keep from being bored to death. Since this activity did not quite fit my idea of a paid vacation in paradise, I requested and received permission from the base commander, Colonel Jack

Bentley, to build a beach club in my spare time to try to interest the men in water activities.

When I arrived at the island few people were even swimming because they had been told the waters were infested with dangerous sharks and moray eels. Moreover, there was a standing military order that no one was to eat any fish caught in the local waters because they were said to be poisonous. When I heard this I wondered what kind of paradise I had landed in. While stationed in Honolulu I had bought a mask and fins in anticipation of diving on Johnston Island, and I was eager to try them out, whether the fish were ready or not.

In due course the club was built on the beach and I was ready for action. Casting about for someone who might have accurate knowledge about diving in the local waters, I found one Sam Kahoiwai, the ranking civilian in charge of the island's steam plant and water distillation plant, who was well versed on the subject of diving. A fierce-looking man with a magnificently hooked nose, Sam was half-Hawaiian, half-Apache Indian, and an all-around great fellow. He was in charge of one of the most important functions on the island—converting salt water to several thousand gallons of fresh water a day. When he learned that I was interested in the sport of free diving, he offered to take me out in his small boat and introduce me to the offshore reefs.

It was an unforgettable introduction. On the morning we went we carried fins, masks and a Hawaiian sling speargun Sam had made from a segment of bamboo and a length of rubber tubing. While it was against regulations to eat any fish from the ocean, there was no regulation against spearing them. Sam said that the natives paid no attention to the order and ate the fish anyway.

"I don't think it bothers anyone anymore," said Sam, "but before you came to the island several people got deathly sick from eating local fish. I never figured it out. They were the same fish we get at home and they are never poisonous."

How curious to hear that such familiar species as red snappers, groupers, even sharks—fish I had harpooned for my family and we had enjoyed eating many times through the years—were now considered poisonous in this tropical paradise. Was this the rotten apple in Eden? Maybe I would see something offshore that would explain the mystery.

As we motored out to the reef, aware this would be my first dive in tropical Pacific waters, Sam filled me in on all the things I should not do, the species of fish that I was to avoid touching.

"A stonefish looks like something you might see in a bad dream," said Sam. "Lots of thick heavy dorsal spines and a warty hide. This one's particularly bad because he camouflages himself so well. He may look like a clump of mud or debris. But if you accidentally come in contact with any of those spines, you'll think you've been bitten by a rattlesnake." And, according to Sam, there was no known antivenom.

Next in his repertoire of do-nots related to the triggerfish and the surgeonfish—both nasty customers if any close contact was considered. The first dorsal spine of the triggerfish was a long, rigid, awl-like weapon that the fish could flip vertical and lock in place. The only thing that would unlock it was the short second spine, which acted as a trigger. Press it and the first spine would unlock and fold back in place. Apparently this first spine was extremely sharp and could cause considerable damage if erected against any part of a diver's anatomy.

"And watch out for the surgeonfish," cautioned Sam. "He may look harmless but he isn't. They don't call him a surgeon for nothing. He has a short but sharp, scalpel-like spine on each side of his tail that folds forward and out of sight as neatly as the blade of a jackknife when it's closed. But if he gets excited that blade flips out at an angle from his body, and with a swipe of his tail he can slice you up pretty good." Sam wasn't sure whether the surgeonfish's knives were venomous or not, and he had no intention of finding out.

Reaching the place Sam wanted to show me, we moored the boat, donned our diving gear and went over the side into twenty feet of the clearest water I had ever seen. Visibility was at least 200 feet. Everywhere I looked I saw a fantasy world. I had never dreamed it was that beautiful. A forest of table, or umbrella, coral stretched in all directions. Beneath their broad stony branches were pathways of snow-white sand. It was a kaleidoscope of colors. Those moving rainbows were tropical fish, most of which I had never seen before. I had no idea what kind they were.

Sam showed me how to use the Hawaiian sling, a hollow segment of bamboo with a loop of rubber tubing attached to one end. A slender steel spear was slipped into the barrel of the speargun and its butt grasped between the sides of the rubber tubing. You held the bamboo cylinder in one hand while stretching the spear and rubber back with the other, much the way a slingshot operates. When you released the spear it was thrust forward swiftly. If your Kentucky windage was not too far off, the spear usually hit its target.

After a few practice shots I was able to dive down and spear a rather remarkable large oval-shaped fish whose color and markings looked like an abstract artist's nightmare. So elated was I over my lucky shot that I failed to notice Sam frantically waving at me underwater as I recovered the thrashing catch and tried to get him off my spear. I was too absorbed to realize that I had skewered one of Sam's do-not-touch triggerfish—that is, until the beast's dorsal fin sprang up like a small switchblade and almost amputated my finger.

Hence my first lesson in this underwater wonderland: Don't touch anything you're unsure of. If I forgot, all I had to do was look at my profusely bleeding finger to remember.

The next thing Sam pointed out to me underwater was a curious glob hugging the base of one of the coral trees. When Sam made an aggressive move in its direction, the glob disengaged itself and rocketed backward, trailing its long suckered legs behind its now more recognizable bulbous head. It was an octopus.

We followed close on its heels and in the next few minutes saw this remarkable creature shift quickly through different color changes in an effort to camouflage its whereabouts. Since octopuses are Hawaiian delicacies, Sam soon had us playing tag through the rough branches of table coral with every octopus in the neighborhood. Those he speared were brought quickly to the surface, where Sam gave them the coup de grace by putting the octopus's neck in his mouth and biting it sharply to kill the animal. As horrible as the act seemed, it was no time before he had me doing it.

Everywhere I looked the reef abounded with fish. Some I recognized, but most I didn't. Occasionally a shark cruised into view, looked us over and moved on. None seemed dangerous to us. As I looked over that lush landscape with all its colors and virginal populations of fish, I saw no reason on earth why these fish would be poisonous—if indeed they were.

After Sam had introduced me to the fascinating world of the Pacific Ocean reef, I found life there infinitely more interesting than at the officers' club. During my off hours I took every opportunity to go offshore free diving to explore this remarkable new world. Before long I wasn't satisfied until I could get down deeper and stay there longer. To do that I needed scuba equipment and a larger, more powerful speargun.

As soon as I could get away I flew to Honolulu with my pilot buddy, Captain Bob McGann, to buy the gear I needed: an air tank and a big three-rubber arbalete speargun.

Getting air on Johnston Island was no problem. We used the big compressor that inflated the struts on aircraft. Not only were we unfamiliar with the hazards of using scuba but also with the hazards of filling steel tanks with high-pressure air. Again, my guardian angel must have been standing by because the tank never once went off like a bomb or made like a runaway missile. Lacking filters on the compressor, we unknowingly risked getting oil spray in the air we were to breathe. Fortunately, however, it never bothered us. At least we knew enough not to fill the tanks downwind from the compressor's exhaust where the compressor would suck in fumes containing deadly carbon monoxide, a combination that surely would have caused us serious trouble underwater.

Scuba opened up entirely new vistas for me. But it was at least a month before I could interest any of the men on the island to accompany me. Meanwhile I dived alone and managed to harpoon and land a couple of the six-foot sharks we often saw around the reefs. The arbalete proved effective against them—far superior to Sam's homemade Hawaiian sling, which was suitable only for smaller fish. The arbalete could fire a steel harpoon through a two-by-four piece of wood. Seldom did it fail to pierce the extremely tough hide of a shark if I hit him right. I found that if I aimed below the mid or lateral line that ran the length of the body, the hide was soft enough to allow penetration. Usually if I hit them above this line the harpoon would go in only an inch or two, but more often it would bound off the hide. It was necessary to get really close to a shark in order to penetrate at all. But once I learned how, I would shoot them in the gills or the lower body and be successful.

On my first try at sharks I was out about 600 feet among the coral heads when what I suspected was a gray reef shark about six feet long passed close to me. I swung and fired. The harpoon penetrated only about six inches into his body. The shark turned and lunged at me. When I beat him off with the speargun he went over the top of the reef, taking me with him.

Since I refused to let him have my gun and the harpoon did not appear to be tearing out, the shark dragged me at the end of my twenty-five-foot steel spear cable through the roughest kind of coral imaginable. Each of those rock-hard branches with their sharp points and protuberances seemed determined to take a chunk out of me.

In the end the shark broke off the spear at its cable connection and escaped, leaving me to wonder at the wisdom of hanging on to such a critter. Taking stock of my scrapes and bruises, I found that I had also managed to pick up a dozen of the long, slender, black sea urchin spines that punctured me in several places and now burned like fire.

For a few weeks I dived by myself and speared an assortment of fish. Then some of the other men, no doubt realizing that the dangers offshore were not as drastic as they thought, approached me about starting a diving club so they could learn the sport too.

I was delighted with the idea. Before long more than half a dozen men were outfitted with Honolulu masks, fins and Hawaiian slings. When others saw how much fun we were having they also became involved in free diving. Those who knew how taught those who didn't. Pretty soon our diving club had two dozen underwater hunters learning the sport. But the mainstay of the group were the first four divers I trained: Ray Fisher, Tom Pierce, Chaplain Penrod and Fred Litz. These men were able to get away more often than the others and consequently we dived together more frequently. We went out as a group at least once a week and sometimes twice, crowding into our small boat and heading for the reef.

Eventually most of us became adept at being able to free-dive up to forty or fifty feet. Since there were only two scuba tanks on the island, mine and the one belonging to McGann, who seldom was around long enough to use it, most of our dives were with mask and fins. The men learned to hyperventilate on the surface and were soon proficient at diving down and holding their breath up to three minutes.

Whatever eating fish we speared were given to the natives. They had no qualms about their being poisonous and seemed genuinely glad to get them. So far as I knew there were never any incidents of poisoning from the fish we gave them.

One day, however, a plane landed at the island with several scientists from the school of tropical and preventive medicine from a medical college at Loma Linda, California. Among them was Dr. Bruce W. Halstead, who was under a research grant from the National Institutes of Health, the Public Health Service and the Office of Naval Research to study the problem of poisonous reef fish. This was not the first time Halstead had been to the island, not was it the first study scientists had made on the subject.

Shortly after meeting the men I learned that in 1951 Dr. Vernon E. Brock and his associates from the Division of Fish and Game for the Territory of Hawaii made a fisheries survey of the island. During the study they found that local fish poisoning was frequent enough to be a public health hazard. When the scientists collected samples from the inner reef and shipped them to Loma Linda for analysis, the fish were found to be toxic.

In retracing the history of the island the investigators realized that it would be difficult to pinpoint exactly when fish caught in the area became poisonous. But they felt it probably coincided with a similar general outbreak that seemed to have occurred about 1943 in adjacent islands. Subsequently it worked its way through the group with the exception of the Hawaiian Islands, which were apparently not affected. Other areas may have been involved, but the scientists had no record concerning them.

From Captain John T. Martin, who was formerly the base surgeon at Johnston Island, they learned that the first documented case of fish poisoning occurred in August 1950. Outbreaks were thought to have occurred before that but there were no clinical observations on the subject. Fishes caught inside the lagoon were reportedly poisonous while those taken outside the lagoon were supposedly safe for human consumption.

Despite posted warnings and rigid regulations at Johnston Island prohibiting eating reef fishes, there were still periodic outbreaks of fish poisoning among both the civilian and military personnel. According to Halstead's findings, in 1950 and 1951 there were approximately twenty outbreaks of fish poisoning. Most were among the native civilian workers who had been brought to Johnston Island from the Hawaiian Islands. The patients were violently sick to their stomachs, experiencing nausea, vomiting, diarrhea and abdominal pain over a period of two to three hours. This was accompanied by peculiar sensory problems in which anything warm felt cold and anything cold felt warm. Some patients complained of a tingling sensation in and about the mouth. Sometimes they suffered severe prostration or muscular cramps. Most patients recovered within a few days.

In trying to find some reason for the toxicity of the fish, the scientists spent considerable time in 1951 studying the layout of the reefs, the algal growth, the fish populations in various areas, the condition of the coral and the general environment of the waters adjoining the island.

After completing their study they were still no closer to the answer. However, they noted that off the west end of the island wreckage had been pushed into the ocean and that the shoreline was a dump, littered with scrap metal. The twelve-foot-deep water in this area was murky, the bottom covered with coral boulders, rubble and wreckage. Since this was not a natural environment, the scientists wondered if fish feeding around the wreckage might become toxic. At the time they were unable to prove it. All they could say with any certainty was that apparently any species could become toxic if the proper environmental conditions were present.

No one knew exactly what environmental conditions created this strange phenomena. The investigation simply revealed that approximately 47 percent of the reef fish tested from Johnston Island at that time were toxic. The toxicity of any species was variable, but the scientists felt it was all part of the general outbreak that started in 1943 at Palmyra Island and later involved other Midway islands. Cause and exact distribution of the problem were unknown. And, as a final unfortunate note to the Johnston Island investigation, Dr. Vernon Brock was savagely attacked by a ten-foot-long moray eel he had tried to spear as a specimen. Suffering a severely crushed and lacerated hand, the scientist was rushed to Honolulu for immediate medical attention.

Now Dr. Halstead and his companions had returned to see what more could be learned about the problem of fish toxicity in the area. When he heard that our group was successfully spearing reef fish he asked us to help his team gather specimens, especially the more difficult to get reef sharks and moray eels.

That was all the encouragement we needed. From then on we launched ourselves into the shark-hunting and moray-eel business with a vengeance.

3

~~~~~~~~~~~~ *tigers by the tail*

AS SOON AS the others in our spearfishing club heard
about the Halstead project they were anxious to round
up as many sharks and eels as they could find in the reefs.
But most of the men were not that advanced in their
spearfishing, and very few had as yet had any real encounters with large sharks. Everyone had Hawaiian
slings capable of taking small to moderate-size fish, but
they were in no way powerful enough to cope with even
a small shark.

Whenever we went out I always reminded the divers to

use the buddy system and never to let their buddy out of sight. I told them that in the event of a shark attack they should never turn tail and swim away from the animal. They should always face the shark. If the shark made a pass at the diver, only then should he fire his sling to protect himself. But he would be better off using it just to push the shark away. If he had nothing more than a diver's knife, he was to use that. But avoid touching, and then only as a last resort, the shark's denticle-covered hide with bare hands, because once grazed by the rough-er-than-sandpaper shark skin there was a good chance the encounter would draw first blood—the diver's blood —leading to a probably more determined shark attack.

Some of our divers were so new at the sport that they were understandably quite apprehensive about meeting their first sharks. I tried to describe to them what to expect before they ever left the boat. One such diver, Lieutenant Allen Wong, a Chinese-Hawaiian who had never done any shark fishing, seemed to understand all about it . . . right up to the time he came face-to-face with an aggressive shark.

On that particular day Wong, Ray Fisher and four others had joined me for a trip to the reef in the large air-sea rescue lifeboat Colonel Bentley had kindly provided for us. We anchored to the north of the island just inside the reef in about thirty feet of water, where there were many coral heads on the bottom.

The sea was calm and the water clear as we paired up and went over the side to hunt. The men with Hawaiian slings went to work on the smaller species of reef fish while my buddy Ray Fisher and I searched for sharks using scuba and arbaletes.

Oddly enough, on this particular day no matter where we looked we were unable to find any of the trim gray stiletto shapes that we had learned to recognize so well. There seemed to be no sharks in the neighborhood.

Meanwhile the other divers were having good luck shooting a variety of reef fish and small moray eels. Fisher and I swam around searching for sharks until we had used up all our air. We were on our way back to the boat when suddenly one of the men shouted to us, "Hey, you guys! A shark's after Wong!" The man was pointing excitedly to a commotion in the water not far from the boat.

Fisher and I ducked under and saw a chilling sight. Wong was thrashing through the water like a wild man, moving fast but not fast enough. The big gray form was quickly closing the gap behind him.

We swam toward the hapless Wong, thinking that maybe we could drive off the shark before he attacked. But just as we got within a few yards we were horrified to see the shark dart forward and apparently clamp his jaws on Wong's foot.

Wong shrieked in panic. Fisher fired his arbalete and the spear tore into the shark's abdomen. Almost immediately he coughed up the contents of his stomach.

We saw a dark cloud, but it didn't look like blood. We weren't sure how much of Wong's leg had been bitten off along with his flipper, but Wong managed to thrash his way to the boat, where he was quickly helped aboard.

Meanwhile Fisher and I were having our own problems with the shark. It whipped around and came within jaw-snapping reach of both of us, but we butted it away with our arbaletes. Finally it broke off Fisher's harpoon and wobbled off into the blue with the shaft still sticking out of his side.

Hurrying back to the boat we found Wong stretched on the deck, his face the clammy white color of the underbelly of a flounder. Not only was he panicked, he was in shock. I half expected to see the boat splotched with great swatches of red. But close examination revealed that Wong was completely intact and unharmed, except of course for his composure. He had simply lost his flipper.

Fisher and I dived down to the bottom and found it for him. It was ripped and badly tooth-marked all over. We took it back to the boat and showed it to Wong. He stared at it wide-eyed, no doubt thinking what would have happened had the shark been just a few inches closer.

Needless to say Lieutenant Wong never again showed up to go shark hunting with us.

The incident was unnerving to everyone, but I still felt that had Wong turned and confronted the shark rather than run, the attack would not have occurred. But Wong probably reacted without thinking, which was a normal impulse.

Despite the almost unlimited visibility we had in the water, sharks sometimes had an uncanny way of appearing suddenly beside us before we saw them. Fisher always claimed that half the sharks he ever saw came from behind him. I believe he is right. The sharks to worry about are the ones you don't see.

Six of us were aboard the boat hunting sharks near the inner edge of the barrier reef. I had already collected a four-foot specimen and another shark that would measure around six feet. In an effort to chum the sharks closer to the boat, we harpooned a six-pound mutton snapper and cut it up on the bottom to attract sharks.

I was holding one of these chunks of bait in my hand over my head when out of nowhere a shark swept in and took it away from me. I didn't even see him do it. All I felt was a tug, and when I whirled around a seven-foot shark gulped down the morsel as he made good his getaway. I was thankful it was just the fish and not my hand he was going off with.

More than once in those days I thought how nice it would be to have a rear-view mirror handy when swimming in shark-infested waters. Someone else must have gotten the same idea because today one of the diving accessories is a small mirror that straps on the wrist so a diver can see behind him without turning around. Some beginning ocean divers probably spend most of their time watching that rear-view mirror.

Sharks, we found, were very adroit at sneaking a fish away from us. I would like to think that the shark just mentioned knew the difference between my hand and the fish, and had intentionally selected the latter. One of our divers had a string of fish hanging from his belt as he swam. I saw a shark make a pass at him, and as I swam their way the shark neatly snipped off the stringer and made off with the fish. Quite obviously this diver was also pleased with the shark's selection.

As we became more adept at spearing specimens for Dr. Halstead we learned more about how to handle the underwater creatures we were dealing with. The men spearing small reef fish quickly found that if they did not wish to attract sharks they had to get their quarry out of the water and into the boat as soon as possible. Speared struggling fish acted like a dinner bell to the sharks. Sometimes holding the fish tight to our bodies as we made our way back to the boat prevented the flurry that broadcast the low-frequency sound waves sharks seemed especially tuned in to, the sounds of a fish in trouble.

Since most of the men were free diving, they seldom delayed getting their catches into the boat. Too, they learned quickly how to handle their fish. They knew which species they could grasp by the gills to guide to the surface and which they should never touch this way, such as grouper or sea bass. Grouper gills are lined with hundreds of tiny sharp teeth that might let your hand go in, but they hold it tight when coming out. Hands that get out of a grouper's gills once never go in again.

I soon learned that well-speared sharks could be more quickly subdued if I swam in, grasped the embedded spear shaft in my left hand to guide the shark's head away from me, and wrapped my other arm around his body. This maneuver resulted in some pretty wild rides reminiscent of my early encounter with the shark on Cortez Bridge. These Johnston Island sharks were so reluctant to give up that even with a mortal wound they would roll, twist, spin and buck wildly in an attempt to keep me from steering them to the surface. If they were large and more difficult to control, I would release the spear, grab them by the tail and go for a ride until the shark tired.

I knew this was a dangerous sport and I didn't recommend it to the other divers. But having had a similar experience before with a shark, I knew they could not reach back and get me as long as I held my body in line with their tail.

Until now all our activities had been inside the reef in a moderate depth of water. Beyond the reef, where the water rapidly dropped to greater depths, there were larger and, we suspected, more fierce sharks, big ones that might even be too much for our arbaletes.

One day I accidentally had the opportunity to meet some of these sharks outside the reef. We had been working our normal area when the tide started going out. From where we were the water emptied from the inner reef through a narrow slot in the coral wall, a slender passage too narrow for our boat to negotiate.

It was late afternoon and I decided to make one more dive before we left. As I swam down along the inner edge of the reef I got too close to the narrow pass and the outgoing tide caught me. It was too strong to swim against and I was forced through the narrow coral outlet.

This was a dangerous place to be. In calmer water I had seen large sharks pass through there before. But now the water was white with turbulence; I could see nothing around me. If a shark were beside me now I wouldn't have known it. I held my speargun crossways, not only to avoid any gobbler that might be making the trip with me but also to avoid the rough coral walls that I was passing at high speed.

In seconds I was sucked through the passage and spit out into the deep water of the open ocean, where the current immediately slacked off.

The surrounding depths were clear and blue. As I looked down I counted fourteen large sharks cruising beneath me about 100 feet away. I felt a little conspicuous. There was no way in the world that I could swim back through that inlet. The tide was still sweeping out and there was less than a foot of water over the ragged top of the reef, which at that point was about 250 feet across.

Since the inlet was too narrow for the boat to go through, no one was coming to my rescue. Dusk was moving in so quickly that even now I could barely see the boat on the other side of the reef some 300 feet away.

I yelled as loud as I could and waved my arms to attract their attention, but there was little they could do. The only pass wide enough to get the boat through was about three miles southwest of the diving area. If I swam there it would be another mile swim back to the island. By then it would be long after dark, not the best time to be swimming with sharks. I couldn't make it.

As these thoughts raced through my mind I kept a wary eye on the sharks milling around below me. One beautiful creature looked to be at least fifteen feet long. But he seemed less interested in my presence than some of the smaller sharks. I've noticed this before. Whenever a number of sharks are around a large bait, the smaller and younger sharks are far more aggressive than the older and probably wiser members. The latter remain in the background as if waiting for the youngsters to start some kind of feeding action. Once it starts, the big boys move in swiftly and often snatch the lion's share of the prize from the small sharks.

It seemed that we were about to get into the first phase of that game. I cursed my luck in having only a single spear with no cable attached. The small sharks circled closer. Their movements indicated they were working up nerve to see what manner of morsel the tide had cast in their midst.

The bravest of the lot, a five-footer, finally cranked up enough courage to make a pass at me. As he tore off with my spear in his side, I hoped he had satisfied his curiosity.

That left me the empty arbalete for protection. I was wondering how I could lash my dive knife to the gun's barrel when someone suddenly said, "Hey, Bill! What's up?"

I spun around, surprised to see one of my diving buddies behind me. "What the devil are you doing out here, Pierce!"

"Thought you might need some help. We heard you yell. No one else in the boat would come out through the reef."

"Oh great! Now that makes two of us stranded out here. But thanks, ol' buddy. Except for our friends downstairs it was already getting a little lonesome."

"Yeah," said Pierce. "I don't much like the looks of them either. What'll we do now?"

I told him we had two choices. We could swim for the boat pass, hoping someone would come out in the rescue boat down there and pick us up. Or we could try going over the top of the reef the way we had sometimes seen sharks do it. This was always a peculiar sight because when the tide ran out there was hardly any water over the reef. Yet large sharks would actually propel themselves up on top of the coral until almost their entire bodies were out of the water and then, using a head-swinging movement, squirm their way across the broad expanse until they finally splashed over inside the reef. I couldn't imagine why they would choose this rough route unless sometimes the velocity of the tide through the narrow cut was too strong even for them to negotiate.

In either event this seemed to be our only feasible route. But since we didn't even have gloves with us it meant that we were in for a pretty tortuous trip. The upper surface of the reef was riddled with deep pools, pockets, holes and crevices, which made walking over it virtually impossible. The place was loaded with all sizes of moray eels not to mention the mine fields of bristling black sea urchins ready to stick their hatpin quills into anything that touched them.

As unappealing as it was, it seemed that making a kind of swimming crawl over the top of the reef was our only hope. I told Pierce what kind of problems we could expect. His only comment was, "Let's get it over with, Bill."

So we started. The crossing was painful enough, but if it had been any darker it would have been a lot more painful. At least we could see to avoid the more treacherous holes where moray eels with open jaws eyed us malevolently for our intrusion. Luckily we had no bad encounters with them; unluckily we couldn't say the same for the sea urchins blocking our way. In the eight-inch-deep water we squirmed and pushed our way through them, parrying the living pincushions aside with our arbaletes and trying not to touch them. It was a weird feeling being so close to these animals and seeing the spines turn in our direction, moving in the water like long, sharp, black fingers reaching for us. Some of the urchins were impossible to avoid. When their brittle needles pierced our flesh neither of us hid our feelings. In fact, as I recall, we alternately cussed and yelped our way across every foot of that hellish 250-foot reef.

Like the sharks we somehow wallowed our way through. And many a time during that crawl we wished we had hides as tough as the sharks that had made that trip.

Watching our progress from the boat, the other divers moved it closer to the reef to pick us up. When we reached them, willing hands hauled our scraped and bleeding carcasses aboard. By then it was about dark and we headed back to the island, extremely relieved that we were not still in the water on the other side of the reef waiting for the swift shadows to close in on us.

After seeing what was out there I was anxious to get beyond the reef again, preferably in a boat. Soon we were making the trip in the large air-sea rescue craft. Normally we would go out trolling for fish whenever there were nondivers aboard, which was a rule of the base. Once in awhile only the divers took out the boat.

On fishing trips we trolled for big fish and occasionally caught them. But we seldom landed them intact because of the sharks. They trailed behind the boat—we could see them some distance beyond our baits—and whatever fish we hooked never lasted long because of these hungry predators. The minute a big fish struck, a shark would flash in and start chomping him off piece by piece. We would feel the tugging and reel in fast, speeding up the boat to try and save the fish. But the sharks were too swift for us. They always got their quarry, sometimes chopping them off just as we pulled them out of the water right at the boat. Often all we had left was the head of a big fish. Pretty discouraging business.

On one rare occasion I was able to fight and land a 400-pound yellow-fin tuna without it being mutilated by sharks, which surprised us all. I have no idea why they failed to get this particular fish unless it happened that they were busy elsewhere.

We butchered the fish and wanted to give it to the mess hall so it could be served to everyone on the island. But Colonel Bentley was so afraid it was poisonous, even though it had been caught outside the reef, he forbade us to eat it. The fish finally ended up with a group of Hawaiians who cut off great chunks for themselves. At least they got a good feed out of it.

I was losing so many spearguns and spears that I decided to build a CO_2 gun. By coupling a piston to a large CO_2 tank and adding a trigger, I found that it fired a shaft with tremendous velocity. Since the CO_2 tank was half the size of my seventy-two-cubic-foot air tank, I had enough carbon dioxide to fire harpoons repeatedly for hours. Many, of course, would be lost, so I made a good supply of heavy spears at the base machine shop. Now I was ready to try spearfishing beyond the reef and find out what could be done with those large sharks.

The first trip was mostly exploratory. Ray Fisher and Fred Litz joined me. Having already seen what sharks could do to catches we made on our trolled lines, I was curious to see how they attacked them.

Fisher and Litz dropped me off in deep water with my CO_2 gun, then baited hooks and trolled them past me while I watched to see what happened below.

By the third pass the baits had picked up a following of ten sharks trailing behind about thirty yards; probably the same following the boat usually had when anglers came out to troll.

On the third pass a crevalle jack came out of the blue

and grabbed Fred Litz's bait. It happened so close to me I saw everything—the jack slanting off at an angle, diving deep, cleaving his quivering, flat shape through the water like a wedge, then abruptly cutting back and driving to the farthest point he could get in the opposite direction.

The fish made three or four lightning-fast runs, fighting hard against the reel's drag, when suddenly the sharks were there.

It was instantaneous, like someone throwing a switch. One second they were lagging behind, then bam! They were hurtling past me like torpedoes zeroing in on the wildly ricocheting jack. I never saw such speed.

The first one hit the target as if he had been programmed to it. His jaws got half the fish; his cohorts, the rest. In seconds a mad melee of feeding erupted around me. Suddenly I wished I was in the boat.

It was over almost as soon as it began. The sharks peeled off but were still obviously excited over the slaughter. One of them turned and came toward me. Whether he was just checking me out or coming in to see if I was just as tasty as the jack I'll never know. When he was in range I pulled the trigger of my CO_2 gun and he disappeared in a welter of ejected bubbles.

Even when I could see again I never knew whether I hit the shark or he just evaporated in all those bubbles. Anyway he was gone. And as I looked back on the scene again I saw the group of sharks in their normal position, silently bird-dogging the trolled baits as if nothing had happened.

The following week Fisher and a couple of nondivers joined me on another trip outside the reef. This time we would still-fish for sharks. I wanted to see how a shark would go for a lifeless bait hanging on a hook in the water.

When we reached deep water I went overboard with the gas gun but no scuba. Instead of anchoring we let the boat drift. The water was so clear and blue it was like swimming through liquid sky. Shafts of sunlight reached down through the depths to dapple the white sand bottom 200 feet below. From my high vantage point I counted at least thirty sharks lazily swimming near the bottom.

Fisher rigged the deep-sea rod and dropped the bait over the side. The thick slab of bloody bonito skewered on its hand-size hook dangled about thirty feet below me for only two or three minutes before I saw a heavy-bodied shark detach itself from the crowd below and angle up to inspect it.

The closer it got the bigger it became. Its slightly yellow cast and almost equal-size dorsal fins identified it as a lemon shark about ten feet long. Paying no attention to me, the shark slowly circled the bait a few times, then moved in to engulf it. There was no furious strike the way there had been with the struggling jack. Just a casual look-over, then an equally casual pickup of the bait.

As the big creature moved off with the bonito in its jaws I expected to see sudden fireworks. But they never came. Of all things, the shark dropped the bait!

Again it circled. This time, however, the shark seemed slightly annoyed. The circles grew more erratic. Then I saw something strange: the lemon shook its head several times. The movement rippled through its entire body as if the animal were trying to work itself into a furor over that piece of meat hanging in the center of its circles. Several times this happened while the shark went round and round, then abruptly it snatched the bait and dashed off.

The shark was moving faster than before, but when Fisher set the hook, leaning back on the big rod and driving the barb into the animal's jaw, it paused just long enough to realize, I imagine, that something was not quite right with its breakfast. Then it tore off into the blue.

Fisher and the others rode it out in the boat while I swam some distance away, watching for the shark to reappear. Finally I saw it moving at high speed deep down near the bottom, a fast-moving shadow that had now attracted a host of other shadows. The whole tribe of sharks tagged along behind the one Fisher had hooked, wondering perhaps why their companion was acting so strangely.

Gradually Fisher gained more line and the action drew closer. The shark ricocheted from one sizzling run to another, which kept me moving just as quickly to avoid Fisher's line. Underwater I couldn't see the wire-taut dacron line, but I knew if I was hit by it during one of the shark's speed runs I'd look like sliced salami.

Finally Fisher got the lemon alongside the boat and was having trouble dispatching it. They had the shark hoisted partway out of water on the leader cable but it was thrashing wildly, showering everyone in the launch.

"Hey Bill," called Fisher, "you want to ride this devil? We gotta do something to calm him down or he'll shake the boat apart!"

I swam alongside and grabbed the shark by the tail. It

promptly slammed me against the boat hard enough to have cracked some ribs. Scrambling to avoid a repetition, I suddenly found myself astride the animal's back, my legs wrapped around its body, my hands locked in a death grip on its pectoral fins. Great shades of Cortez Bridge, here I was again!

Immediately I regretted my move. The shark went wild, crashing, banging, bucking. Over the sound of our bodies thudding repeatedly against the hard hull of the launch, I caught snatches of Fisher shrieking for me to do something more than just go for a ride. I got the impression that he wanted me to kill the beast.

Somehow I managed to get hold of my dive knife without falling off. Then, in the best Hollywood tradition, I reached around underneath the shark and jabbed my razor-sharp blade into its belly.

Two more tentative jabs later I knew the well-honed blade had not gone in. About the time I was trying to figure out how to disengage myself from the animal without getting into any more serious trouble, the blade suddenly pierced the shark's tough hide and ripped a two-foot gash.

Overhead one of the guys on the boat yelped, "Jeeze, look at all the little sharks!"

Swimming through the blood and guts around me were half a dozen sharks about twelve to fifteen inches long. Then I realized that Fisher's lemon was no gentleman—it was a pregnant female whose fully developed offspring were tumbling out of my Caesarean section one after another. Needless to say the patient did not respond well to my treatment.

I was immediately bucked off. Staring down into the

water I saw at least a dozen perfect miniature sharks swimming quickly away from the scene of their impromptu birth. What discouraged me from further observation was the sight of full-grown sharks just below me streaking in to devour them. The last thing I saw before rapidly exiting the water was sharks snapping at everything in sight, the drifting offal as well as the swift-swimming offspring of the big lemon. Possibly some escaped; I didn't wait around to find out.

Seconds later, back in the boat, we cut loose the female. For a moment the sea boiled and surged around the boat. Then the corpse sank in a seething mass of sharks engaged in a feeding frenzy. As we watched everything dissolve into the quiet blue depths, I could only hope that the female's final contribution to the pack had helped buy time for at least a few of her pups to escape.

4

~~~ morays and other mischief

ALL THE FISH and eels we collected for Dr. Halstead, including sharks up to six feet long, were frozen in the base freezer, then sent to him in Loma Linda, California, for analysis.

Spearing specimens of small to medium-size reef fish was easy, even for the least experienced divers in our group. Spearing sharks was more risky, and usually only our most experienced divers such as Fisher, Pierce and Litz helped me with them. Moray eels were something else again. The inner reef waters proliferated with these unusually large, ill-tempered creatures. It seemed as if every hole in the reef held one or more of them. Ray Fisher's first experience was typical of the way most of the divers on Johnston Island got started.

Shortly after he arrived on the island and saw the diving possibilities, Fisher bought a secondhand mask, fins and a Hawaiian sling for five dollars. With these he was soon getting parrot fish and triggerfish.

One day he and another novice diver named Cozad were trying their luck alongside the beaching ramp early one morning. The ocean was choppy and the water unclear. But while diving down along one of the ledges, Fisher noticed a pair of eyes looking at him from a honeycombed coral formation. Repeatedly he dived down, put his face close to the opening and tried to see what manner of creature owned the eyes. But each time he was unable to tell. So he put the end of his spear in the hole and fired, scoring a hit. Immediately the shaft thrashed wildly.

Thinking he had hit an octopus, Fisher tried several times to pull the creature from the hole, but without luck. Since he saw no ink discharged, he thought perhaps he had a fish instead of an octopus.

Cozad joined him. After trying to free the spear he surfaced and said, "I think I see part of your monster sticking out of one of those other holes."

"Shoot it," said Fisher.

Cozad dove down and shot what he had seen. His spear thrashed as wildly as Fisher's. Both men now wrestled with their respective spears, trying to get the monster into the daylight.

When fifteen minutes had passed and neither was successful, Fisher swam ashore, got a five-foot pry bar from the boathouse and returned with it.

Using this to break away the coral, the men finally saw what they had. Their startled eyes met those of a big moray eel. Fisher had speared him behind his head while Cozad had speared him in the tail. Since the eel was still putting up a good scrap, Fisher terminated the affair with the pry bar. Then they freed Cozad's spear and pulled the eel from the hole. The moray measured over five feet long.

The eel population was so heavy around Johnston Island that every time we went out, someone felt sure they would spear a world-record eel. Lord knows we never had trouble finding them; it was just a matter of determining what the biggest of the big would be. Like the sharks, the eels were often there whether we expected them or not.

One day one of the divers shot a red snapper with a Hawaiian sling. The fish disappeared under the coral and we were looking for it. I spotted a moray eel and shot him. When we pulled the eel from the coral we found another spear sticking out of his mouth. The eel had swallowed the red snapper, spear and all.

Another day, Ray Fisher shot an eel in a coral head. Since we couldn't get the eel out, we tied Fisher's gun to the boat and set the boat adrift. Using the pry bar, McGann and I broke away the coral to get at the eel.

We were free diving, and during one of our breathing breaks on the surface McGann said, "I think I see part of the eel in another hole. I'll put a spear into him and see if I can get him out."

He dived, shot the eel and pulled it from the hole

without any trouble. But it was not the same one Fisher had shot. We continued breaking away the coral. While I was working with the pry bar, Fisher saw a moray's head sticking out of the coral near me. He tapped me on the arm and pointed it out to me. I picked up my gun and shot it.

This one I boated without any trouble. But again it was not Fisher's eel.

Another eel was seen and collected, and then finally we got the first one Fisher had shot. We had gotten four morays over four feet long out of a coral head no larger than a double bed. One thing was certain: Dr. Halstead would have no shortage of moray specimens.

Free diving later in the week, Fisher and I swam over what had to be a moray-eel apartment house. It was a well-like hole about five feet wide and twenty feet deep that went down into the porous limestone. As we peered into this natural formation it looked like a snake pit. Heads of moray eels stuck out at various depths all the way down to the bottom of the hole.

I was curious to see this at close range, so I dove down into the pit, staying away from the walls as much as possible, and swam straight down the middle of the shaft.

At the bottom I stopped and looked up toward the two other divers on the surface. It was a weird sensation, like being at the bottom of a well and looking up to see a dozen snakes with their heads and bodies reaching out a foot or two from the walls. The eels presented a more fearsome sight than I had anticipated. At that moment I regretted having made the dive.

I stayed down as long as I could and then, with lungs

aching for air, pushed off from the bottom and came spiraling up through the gauntlet of moray eels.

Why one or more of them didn't move out of their niches to investigate me more closely I'll never know. But they were content to let me alone, and on this particular day I respectfully did likewise with them.

The Johnston Island morays were not always so timid in our presence. On a few occasions, without any molestation, the eels came out into the water and made aggressive passes at us. The few times I saw this the eels were fended off and usually shot to avoid repetition. But it was an unnerving experience.

Muraena is the name given to the whole group of moray eels that frequent tropical and subtropical seas of the world. About ninety species are known. All of these eels are characterized by a small gill opening and, unlike other eels, no trace of pectoral fins. Their dorsal and anal fins are continuous around the tip of the tail. Lacking scales but possessing long sinuous bodies, pointed heads and a large mouthful of sharp backward-angled teeth, morays have such reptilian appearances and dispositions that they have often been called "rattlesnakes of the reef." Some are plain colored, others brightly spotted with vivid contrasting colors enabling them to easily fit in with the dappled light-and-dark patterns of the reefs. The mouth of the moray is a fearsome thing to behold. It is large, extending well behind the eye. The thick, sharp teeth continue back into its throat, where they become part of a floating jaw containing many hooked teeth. When morays open their jaws wide in the act of devouring a fish, you can see their floating jaws chewing and working the fish down into the gullet.

In the Marquesas Keys, I rode a lemon shark during experiments for the Cape Haze Marine Laboratory. *(Photo courtesy William M. Stephens)*

Diving deep with the lemon shark, I watched for evidence of the dye tracer the animal had been injected with prior to the experiment. *(Photo courtesy William M. Stephens)*

Shark teeth appear as handful of black triangles, later to be sold or made into jewelry.

Left: One of my offshore explorations in the late 1950's resulted in finding large leg bones of a prehistoric animal. My small rubber raft helped bring in a variety of fossil bones and teeth. *(Photo courtesy William M. Stephens)*

Co-author Bob Burgess and I came ashore after a search for fossil shark teeth off Venice Beach. Note the size of the teeth in my nylon bag. *(Photo courtesy Sarasota* Herald Tribune)

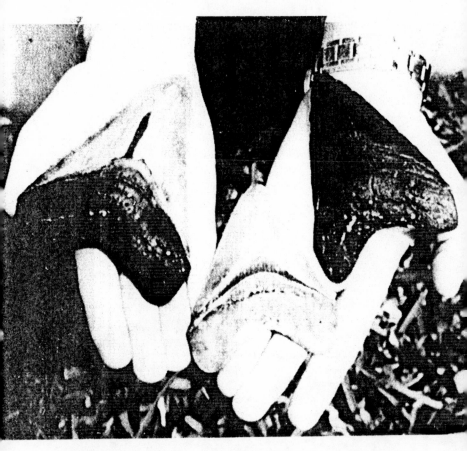

Hand-sized fossil shark teeth found off Venice Beach once belonged to the 20-million-year-old prehistoric relative of today's great white shark.

Hosing down a large bull shark on the Cape Haze shark-catching boat for the ride back to the laboratory.

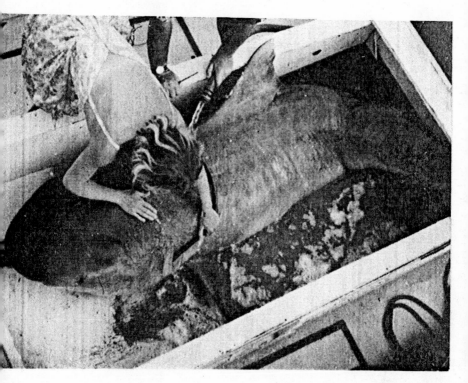

While working as a shark-catcher for the Cape Haze laboratory
a twelve-foot four-inch tiger shark that made a sizeable contri-

I helped Dr. Eugenie Clark measure one of my biggest catches—
bution to the lab's lively shark population.

Left: Beside Warm Mineral Springs I examine some of the human remains recovered from the springs in the early years of my exploration there. The bones proved to be those of early man carbon-dating from 6,000 to over 10,000 years old. *(Photo courtesy William M. Stephens)*

Above: Here I hold the controversial skull containing brain material that was uncovered from the depths of the spring during the television filming. *(Photo courtesy William M. Stephens)*

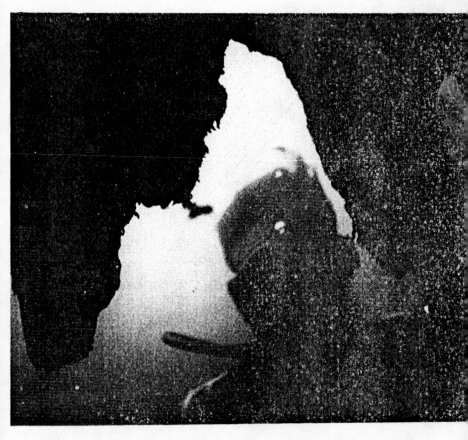

I was amazed to find formations underwater in the springs, *above*, that could only be ancient stalactites. *(Photo courtesy William M. Stephens)*

Right: A depth gauge showed that the stalactites of Warm Mineral Springs are twenty-five to thirty feet beneath the present surface.

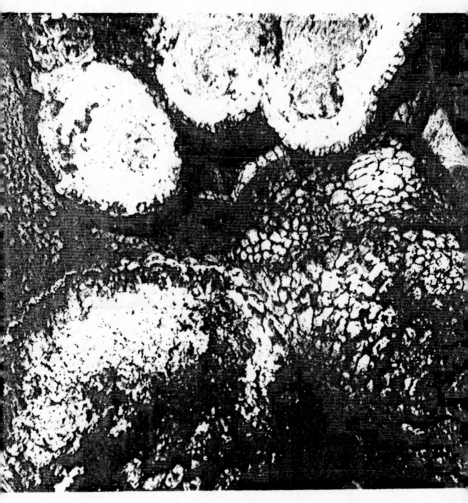

Closeup photographs of broken stalactites beneath the ceiling of Warm Mineral Springs show the growth rings of the formations that formed when the sea level was much lower thousands of years ago.

During the excavation of the 10,000-year-old skull from Warm Mineral Springs, underwater archaeologist Wilburn "Sonny" Cockrell had to remove several huge rocks covering the burial site. Here, I tie off one of several fifty-five-gallon drums used to lift a four-ton boulder from the site.

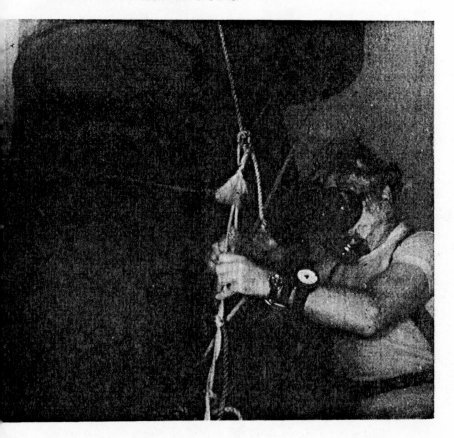

My wife, Shirley, helps me arrange some of the ancient remains
that were recovered from the depths of Warm Mineral Springs
in an effort to interest qualified archaeologists in the site. *(Photo
courtesy Liliane Johnson)*

No one had to remind any of our divers about the dangers of reaching their hands into dark holes in the reef to recover speared fish. The island's folklore contained ample tales of native divers caught in the vicelike jaws of giant moray eels until they drowned. Whether these stories were fact or fiction, we well knew that pulling a hand loose from the bite of a moray was a sure way to lose a pound of flesh.

Most books about marine eels say they are relatively shy creatures with nocturnal habits. But in the reefs around Johnston they had no fear of emerging from their holes and venturing out to feed. We were all used to seeing the eels emerge from their coral crannies to sample one or more of the fish we had cut up on the bottom to attract sharks. We understood this kind of behavior, but for one of them to approach a diver when there was no fish in the water nearby seemed to be an aggressive act on the part of the eel.

On one such occasion Ray Fisher, Chaplain Penrod and I were out among the coral heads hunting eels when a moray about six feet long headed for the chaplain. He saw it just in time to beat it off with his Hawaiian sling. But the eel was as stubborn as some of the sharks we had speared. He kept coming back for more, repeatedly striking at Penrod as if he refused to leave until he had a bite of the good chaplain. Finally we harpooned the eel, but Penrod was pretty shaken by the incident.

On nearby Sand Island there lived a master sergeant who was in charge of communications. Apparently the man had had serious marital problems because he had become a misogamist, a loner who made no bones about disliking people in general. Of course the Sand Island duty was right up his alley; he had the whole place to himself. Often we saw him swimming around the island, and when we went there and spoke to him he told us he would appreciate it if we didn't bother his sharks. "They're my pets," he said.

Another of the sergeant's pets was a big moray eel that lived under the boat dock. Every day at a certain time the sergeant would come down to the dock and hand feed his pet moray. The eel would come to the water's surface and take the food out of his hand. One day, after several months of this kind of taming, the eel must have had a larger appetite than usual: he not only took the food from his benefactor's hand, but he took the hand as well.

Suddenly the sergeant forgot about his dislike for people and put out a fast radio call for help. He was brought to the hospital to treat what was left of his horribly lacerated hand.

Only once on Johnston was I ever attacked by a moray. It happened when a group of us were out hunting sharks. I had dived down toward a coral head and suddenly saw a big moray swimming up to meet me.

There was no misunderstanding his intention. He kept coming straight toward me with his jaws wide open. His body was as thick as my thigh, and with the underwater distortion he looked at least eight or nine feet long—the largest moray I had ever seen. His body was a series of curves undulating through the water like a long brown Oriental dragon kite.

As I dove down to meet him I was struck by the thickness of his flanks, but my main attention was on that ugly humpbacked reptilian head with its beady eyes and mouthful of teeth.

There is only one safe place to shoot a moray eel—straight through the head. Hit him anywhere else and he may slither the length of your spear cable and take his revenge on you.

With my moray the target was too big to miss. When the eel closed his toothy mandibles for the last time, it was not, as he hoped, on some part of my anatomy. He crunched down on the shaft of my spear entering the roof of his mouth and coming out the back of his head.

His broad serpentine body inscribed a series of graceful loops through the water before tying themselves into a constantly coiling and uncoiling monstrous knot on the shaft of my spear.

Gingerly I guided the writhing mass to the surface, threw my gun into the boat and climbed aboard. Then I hauled the catch over the side and examined it. The moray was one of the biggest any of us had ever seen.

Later, on the island, we weighed and measured him. He was seven feet, two inches long. Everyone thought it was probably a spearfishing world record. At least it set a mark for our divers to try and beat. So far as I know no one ever speared a larger moray while I was stationed on Johnston. Ray Fisher came the closest a month after I left by spearing and boating a moray eel that measured six feet, eight inches.

Living on an extremely small island in the middle of an extremely large ocean makes a man tend to pay attention to the details of his environment, the small things on his little speck of land as well as the things the sea sometimes leaves on his watery doorstep. It was this curiosity that made me notice small pieces of pumice rock that had drifted into the lagoon at Johnston. Pumice rock indicated some type of volcanic activity. But since we had no report of any such thing, where did the pumice come from?

I gathered some samples and sent them on to the University of Hawaii in Honolulu, asking them the same question. I thought that if it were possible to find out how long it took this pumice to float into our lagoon, then trace it to its source, we could find out where this deep underwater activity must have occurred.

Back came a letter from marine biologist Dr. Maxwell Doty, who expressed interest in knowing more about the pumice. "When was it first found?" he asked. "How long has it been coming in?"

I wrote Dr. Doty that it had first been noticed on the island about the middle of April 1953, and that at the time large quantities of particles up to half an inch in diameter were seen floating in the lagoon. Most fragments were covered with a green substance resembling algae. Toward the end of June larger masses up to ten inches in diameter were found. These often carried well-developed barnacles. The main drift of pumice ceased in August, but I told him that a considerable amount of the material still remained on the windward beaches.

We corresponded frequently and I mentioned to Dr. Doty the kind of things we had been doing on the reef.

Although the mystery of the pumice rock was never solved, not long after that Dr. Doty and two companions, Jan Newhouser and Dr. Marvin Gilmartin, flew over to Johnston Island, where I had an opportunity to meet them. Dr. Doty was quite interested in sea turtles around the island. Apparently, until then, no one knew exactly what the turtles ate. Dr. Doty asked us to collect some turtle specimens for him so that he could gain some information from analysis of their stomach contents. His companions were also interested in botanical matters— Newhouser in the seaweed and terrestrial plants and Gilmartin in establishing mangrove growth along the north shore.

During our subsequent diving expeditions we learned that the turtles were feeding on large beds of sea grass in certain areas near the island that provided rich pastures for them. When Dr. Doty asked us to capture some of these animals for him, we temporarily ceased our specimen-gathering activities for Dr. Halstead and went after turtles.

This endeavor was not too appealing to us because of the need to kill the huge, slow-moving beasts. When necessary we did it as swiftly as possible by diving down, spearing them, then hauling the carcass to the surface for collection by the boat. The shells were dried and given to servicemen who wanted them as souvenirs. The meat was distributed to the natives, who were pleased to get it for preparing their tasty turtle stews. The stomachs were frozen and sent by air to the University of Hawaii for analysis by Dr. Doty and his associates.

As for ourselves, we wanted to try some of the turtle steaks but Colonel Bentley was afraid the turtle meat was poisonous, even though it had come from the deepwater areas outside the reef.

Our only interest was in collecting a few representative samplings of the local turtle population for the scientists at the University of Hawaii. The rest we enjoyed playing with as best one can with a marine animal weighing upwards of 400 pounds. We would dive down, approach them from the rear and climb aboard for a turtle ride, holding on to their shells in the front and the rear, applying pressure to steer them toward the surface. In the course of the wild rides we sometimes almost drowned before getting our charges to the surface for a gasp of air before plunging off on another submarine tour below with our horny-backed friends.

After a number of turtle specimens were shipped to the University of Hawaii, subsequent scientific papers were published on the findings. Again, as far as I know no one was ever poisoned from eating our turtle meat. Nor did Dr. Halstead know of any cases of turtle poisoning in our part of the Pacific. However, he wrote that such common species as the green sea turtle, the hawkbill turtle and the leatherback turtle, which were not normally poisonous, were for some unknown reason occasionally poisonous in the vicinity of the Philippine Islands, Ceylon and Indonesia under certain mysterious circumstances. The symptoms from eating this poisonous flesh were almost exactly like those of eating poisonous fish from our inner reef waters.

I was also interested to learn that ichthyologist Dr. Eugenie Clark, while doing fisheries research in the Red Sea, reported a case of turtle poisoning in those waters that she had never heard about before. It appears to be a definite case of an animal becoming poisonous from the type of food it ate, a factor that Dr. Halstead and other scientists had long suspected but had not yet proven. Dr. Clark found that this common marine turtle, which was normally a popular native food because it was a large animal weighing up to half a ton, fed almost entirely on fishes, sponges and soft corals. But it was particularly fond of certain jellyfish, a stinging animal that was highly venomous at certain times of the year. Turtles that fed on these jellyfish during these times became poisonous to eat.

The local fishermen apparently knew this and kept the turtles alive and on a poison-free diet for several days. After that they became edible. If a turtle died before the poison-purging period was completed, the natives butchered the animal and tasted the blood from the heart. If it irritated the tongue, the turtle was discarded. If it was not irritating, then the flesh was deemed safe to eat.

I had no doubt that it could happen to the local Johnston Island turtles if conditions were right and they ever cultivated a taste for that certain species of noxious jellyfish.

5

new clues to the riddle of the poisonous fish

AS MUCH AS we were involved with the different sharks around Johnston Island, it may seem surprising that we had so little trouble with them. Many times we were attacked by the sharks we were pursuing, but we expected this as part of our activities. Had there not been a certain amount of risk and danger involved, I doubt we would have found the activity too interesting.

There was no way of anticipating what a shark might

do, but each of us knew that we had to do it to him before he did it to us. That was the challenge. Since our activities went unpublished, none of our shark attack experiences were ever recorded in what came to be known as the International Shark Attack File, the world's most complete data of over 1,600 incidences of shark attacks on man. This file, compiled through the cooperation of the United States Navy in conjunction with the Smithsonian Institution, is presently kept at the Mote Marine Laboratory in Sarasota, Florida, under the directorship of Dr. Perry W. Gilbert, one of the world's foremost authorities on sharks.

Interestingly, the one Johnston Island shark attack mentioned in the file was comparatively mild, much to the relief of the individuals involved, I'm sure. Although it happened over a decade after our shark-hunting activities on the island, what makes this incident unique is the victim's accurate observation of the shark's unusual behavior . . . unusual in the sense that despite our having observed similar reactions, we had not yet identified this behavior as a characteristic attack posture for this particular species.

On December 19, 1965, skin-divers David Fellows and A. E. Murchinson were offshore baiting eel traps with freshly speared fish in twenty feet of water. Suddenly a three-foot gray reef shark came upon the scene.

Fellows decided to spear the shark and started following it closely in a circular path about five feet off the bottom.

Everything was calm during the first lap while Fellows was trying to get close enough to fire his speargun at the shark. Then he noticed a strange thing: "The tailbeat

frequency decreased noticeably and the shark simultane-
ously began to swing the entire anterior portion of the
body side-to-side in greatly exaggerated swimming motion." Swimming above and behind the shark, Fellows
had a good view of this erratic head-swinging behavior.
At this point he had to surface for air.

Glancing down, Fellows saw that the shark had re-
verted to its normal swimming motion and had also risen
in the water mass. It passed directly under Murchinson.
Then it increased its speed, reverting to the same head-
swinging exaggerated manner.

About twenty-five feet away from Fellows the shark
turned and made a speed-run directly at the diver's arm.
Fellows saw it coming and noted that the shark's jaws
were open only about an inch.

Twisting violently aside, Fellows avoided the attack.
The shark passed between his legs, abruptly turned back
and attacked him again, this time encountering the
diver's swim fin. But instead of biting it, the contact
seemed to startle the shark, for it then turned and swam
away.

Years later when I read this account I was interested
in the statements about the shark's erratic behavior. To
a lesser degree it was the same behavior I had witnessed
when the large lemon shark seemed to be working up its
courage to attack the slab of bonito bait we had dangled
on a hook beyond the reef.

Not all sharks give this emphatic warning of an attack,
if indeed that's what it is. However it seems to be quite
common with the gray reef shark, *Carcharhinus menisorrah.*

The only explanation I can give for the lack of any
serious encounters with the sharks we were pursuing in

1953 and 1954 is that we were primarily the aggressors. We never failed to confront the sharks we were after, even when they turned and made passes at us. I firmly feel that had we failed to have something with which to butt the shark away, or had we turned and run from the animal in those instances, we would surely have been bitten.

The one and only time I became a victim of an attack in the waters of Johnston Island, it was by something far more dangerous to divers than sharks.

Our group was out about two miles inside the reef diving for sharks and smaller fish to spear. Colonel Bentley was swimming not over three feet away from me on one side, and two other divers were about five feet away on the other side.

Suddenly I was struck by such excruciating pain across my chest and back that I believe I temporarily passed out. Seconds later I came to groaning painfully. Quickly the other divers got me to the boat and pulled me aboard. They wasted no time getting me back to the island hospital, where the doctors were perplexed about what had actually occurred.

No one had seen anything in the water around me, but by the time I reached the hospital I had a red welt the size of a thick rope encircling my body. It felt as if I were bound tightly by a red-hot chain. The pain was almost unbearable.

Apparently I had swum into some kind of poisonous jellyfish, possibly the torn-off tentacle of a Portuguese man-of-war, the small, purple, balloon-like floating colony of specialized organisms that possesses thin trailing tentacles of stinging cells more than thirty feet long.

Since we had not seen the floating colony, this made me believe I had probably encountered a single tentacle drifting loose and lethal in the water. On contact, thousands of microscopic stinging cells called nematocysts fire their coiled thread-tube hypodermics through the victim's skin and inject their venom. The effect is immediate. How much poison the victim gets, and how susceptible he is to it, determines how much agony he experiences. For some swimmers an encounter with the Portuguese man-of-war has been fatal. In my case, since the tentacle had wrapped around my chest in the area of the heart, the effect was more potent than had it simply touched my arm or leg.

The doctors used a weak solution of ammonia in an effort to counteract the poison. While this was the correct treatment, nothing seemed to stop the intense pain. All they could do was take me to my house, where I suffered for three days until the welt finally disappeared. So I can speak with conviction on the subject of staying well clear of the Portuguese man-of-war. After more than a year of confronting the so-called "dangerous" sharks of the Pacific reefs without receiving so much as a scratch from them, it was ironic that it took part of an animal not much larger than a long thread to put me *hors de combat*. And I didn't even see the critter that did it!

Shock, toxins, sudden damage to the nervous system —these things can sometimes be swiftly crippling or outright destructive to large organisms, be they men or sharks. On two different occasions while spearfishing for sharks I saw something happen that no one has yet been able to explain to me.

Our usual group was out spearfishing for sharks one

day when I shot a nine-foot shark with my arbalete. The spear struck the animal just ahead of his pectoral fin but did not penetrate more than an inch.

Immediately, the shark lost all control of one side of his body and circled around crazily. It was like an individual who had had a stroke that affected only one side of his body.

Another day outside the reef I hit another large shark and again the blow seemed to paralyze him along one side. He dove down into a hole sixty feet deep. Out of curiosity I waited and watched the shark for well over an hour to see if he would recover from his odd behavior. But all he did was flop around in circles. Closer examination revealed that the harpoon had not even entered his body; it had barely nicked his skin. After some time other sharks came into the hole where the big one was wallowing around, attracted, I believe, by his struggles. The wounded shark was at least seven feet long and the smaller sharks worked themselves into a frenzy taking big bites out of his belly. It was a macabre scene to watch.

Later, when I was able to discuss this unusual phenomena with shark experts, they were unable to explain what might have happened. My feeling, however, is that the spear somehow stunned a nerve or a system of nerves that paralyzed the shark's side.

In over a year of shark hunting and periodically collecting fish specimens for Dr. Halstead, observing the fish within the reef and outside it in deeper waters, we saw nothing that we felt even remotely might have caused the fish in these areas to become poisonous, with one exception: a spot close to the southwest end of the island. When we dove in this area we found that the island had been built up there by dumping supplies into the water. Underwater I counted at least 100 electric motors from one horse to maybe fifteen or twenty horse-power. And there was machinery of all kinds: bulldozers, graders, trucks, a variety of motor vehicles—everything had been pushed into the ocean to build up that end of the island to extend the airfield runway.

We had been told that the fish were poisonous in and around the island. When I saw all the junk that had been pushed into the ocean at this point, I wondered if there was any connection between all this corroding metal and the poisoning of the fish. I'm sure there was some oil and gasoline in the motor vehicles when they were shoved into the area. So, in addition to petroleum products, that meant such things as arsenic, lead, copper, tin, zinc and Lord knows what other kinds of chemicals and metals interacting with saltwater. I had no idea how the poisons might be picked up by the fish, but as far as we had seen this was the only area that probably contained contami-nants.

In 1959 Dr. Halstead published *Dangerous Marine Ani-mals* (Cornell Maritime Press, Cambridge, Maryland, 1959). The results of his analysis of our specimens from Johnston Island, combined with all the other aspects of his team's study throughout the Pacific, were summa-rized in this book. On the subject of poisonous fishes, he wrote in part: "The problem of poisonous fishes is an exceedingly complex one and it is quite mystifying to most persons encountering these organisms. One of the difficult things to understand is how a valuable food fish in one locality can be poisonous in another. Neverthe-less, this is the situation that exists. The dual personality of these fishes has caused much confusion both in medical literature and among laymen in the field. The fact that a person may have eaten a particular fish on hundreds of occasions and never found it to be poisonous is no guarantee that this same fish under slightly different circumstances, or in some other locality, will not produce violent intoxication and rapid death.

"The big question is how do fish become poisonous, and what are the factors contributing to the condition? All of the details as to exactly how fishes become poisonous are not known at present. However it is believed that in most instances fishes become poisonous because of their feeding habits. The poison is believed to originate in a marine plant. Plant-eating fishes feed on these plants containing the necessary chemical substances, and the poison is either accumulated or manufactured in the body of the fish. Carnivorous fishes feed on the plant-eating fishes, and the poison is thereby distributed to other groups of fish. As in the case of paralytic shellfish poison, the toxic materials do not affect the fish but are lethal to man when sufficient quantities of the material are eaten."

Dr. Halstead went on to mention that numerous deaths and many illnesses had been reported due to eating sharks and rays. Most illnesses had been caused by eating the livers of these sharks. The marine eels that had been reported in human intoxications were mostly members of the moray eel family, some of which Dr. Halstead said obtained a length of ten feet or more.

All of the species involved in human poisonings were inhabitants of tropical reefs. Most of the reported poisonings occurred from people eating the flesh. Eel soup was a particularly dangerous method of preparation since the poison was readily water-soluble.

This type of poison is called ciguatera to differentiate it from other kinds such as dinoflagellate poison or scombroid poison. In the dinoflagellate poisoning of mollusks or shellfish (the red tide phenomena), microscopic marine animals called dinoflagellates are eaten by the mollusks, and the toxic materials are stored in various parts of the shellfish's body. The poison, while not affecting the mollusk, is lethal to man. Scombroid poison is the toxic substance that occurs when a fish is allowed to spoil.

According to Dr. Halstead there is no way to detect a poisonous fish by its appearance, nor is there any simple test known to detect the poison. The most reliable method the scientists knew of was to inject preparations of tissue extracts into the bellies of mice or to feed samples of the viscera and flesh to cats and dogs and observe their reactions to see if they develop poison symptoms.

In concluding this information in his book, Dr. Halstead said that under survival conditions if one had to eat questionable fish, it was advisable to cut it into thin strips and soak the flesh in several changes of water, because the poison is water-soluble. Then discard the water before cooking the fish. He emphasized that cooking did not destroy or significantly weaken the poison. He also warned that one should be careful of native advice in eating tropical marine fish because it was often erroneous, especially if they had not lived in the area over a period of time. And he warned that one had to be aware that an edible fish in one region might kill you in another.

Further evidence supporting my suspicions that the wreckage off the end of Johnston Island might be contaminating the fish came in findings reported by Dr. Halstead in a paper titled "Toxicity of Marine Organisms Caused by Pollutants," which he presented before the Food and Agriculture Organization of the United Nations Technical Conference on Marine Pollution and Its Effects on Living Resources and Fishing in Rome, Italy, in December 1970. In this study Dr. Halstead said, "Since the days of Thomas (1700) numerous investigators have believed that the ciguatera fish poisoning may be triggered by contamination of the water by such things as copper, various other metallic compounds, dumping of war material, industrial pollutants, shipwreckages, etc.

"The sinking of ships has reputedly caused outbreaks of ciguatera fish poisoning in the Line Islands, central Pacific Ocean. According to all available Public Health reports, poisonous fishes have never been known to occur at Washington Island and Line Islands even though they were found elsewhere in the tropical Pacific islands. The cause of the outbreak was attributed to the sinking of the freighter MS *Southbank* on December 26, 1964. The freighter was heavily loaded with metals and substances which may have contributed to the triggering of the outbreak.

"Many of the common reef fishes of this area were eaten daily by the population without ill effects. Salvage crews had caught and eaten fish with impunity in the immediate vicinity of the wreck up to the time that the portion of the ship containing the main cargo had been completely sunk. Then in August, 1965, the fishes previously edible in the vicinity of the ship suddenly and without warning became ciguatoxic, and the crew members who ate them became violently ill. Similar occurrences elsewhere have been reported many times over the past 100 years."

Some marine biologists feel that the first layer of blue-green algae that forms on this kind of underwater wreckage becomes toxic and is in turn consumed by plant-eating fish. These fish are then eaten by carnivorous fish that are eventually consumed by man, who becomes violently ill from the poison.

What causes the epidemic of fish poisoning to start and then mysteriously come to an end as it does in many of these areas? Some scientists believe that subsequent layers of marine growth are no longer affected by the primary poisons and therefore the fish no longer continue to be poisonous.

Whatever the answer, it appears there is still considerable room for study. As Dr. Halstead wrote in recent personal correspondence, "There are no specific answers. This problem [of ciguatera poisoning] is still unsolved. All we have is a working hypothesis. This problem still exists. The truth of the matter is that the government has never supported sufficient research on this and a vast array of related topics to come up with any realistic answers."

6

~~~~~~~~~~~ *blowing coral, bombs*
and black boxes

SEVERAL MONTHS after being on Johnston Island, pilots told me that from the air they could see the wreckage of a large aircraft underwater about three or four miles from the island. They tried to give me directions to its location, but after repeated unsuccessful attempts to find it, I went up in a DC-3 to have a look at it for myself.

Sure enough it was out there. In the pale blue-green water its shadowy shape looked like a huge shark with stubby pectoral fins. Later I learned that it was a C-54 that had crashed on takeoff from Johnston Island with a load of passengers during World War II. As far as I could learn, no divers had ever visited the wreckage.

Once we got better bearings, Fisher and I and a couple of other divers finally found it with the air-sea rescue boat. It was in twenty feet of water.

We dove down and looked it over. The cabin and part of the fuselage were still relatively intact. Fisher eased himself down through the plane's smashed front end and saluted me from the pilot's seat. His presence disturbed a small cloud of sediment that rose up around him like smoke, as if the forward compartment was smoldering. Fanning it away with one hand, Fisher pantomimed radioing frantically for help with the other, grasping his regulator like an imaginary microphone.

Nodding approval, I made a tour of the wreckage. Some of the engines had torn loose from the wings and rolled down into the coral with their props still on. One of the props had come loose from an engine and was embedded in the coral. Since I knew that the plane had gone down during World War II, this was interesting. It was now 1953 and in the intervening time the coral had grown five or six feet thick until just the blade of the prop protruded from it. It was a good indication of how rapidly coral grows in the unpolluted waters of the tropical Pacific.

I swam back toward the tail of the plane and made my way into the passenger cabin through the rear baggage compartment. The first thing I ran into was a shark!

He woke up and saw me about the same time my eyes adjusted to the dim light and I saw him. It was a big nurse shark that probably thought he had found the ideal place to snatch an undisturbed nap.

A split second after the shock of recognition the water exploded in a cloud of sediment as we both scrambled for exits. In my mind's eye I had a fleeting vision of us both getting caught trying to squeeze through the same hole. Fortunately the shark found another—he went straight out through the side of the fuselage, enlarging a hole that was already there and leaving nothing behind but a spiraling trail of sediment to mark his hasty departure.

Once things settled, I looked around the dim cabin interior again. The fuselage was sheared off at floor level. I found a brogan shoe lying there and hoped its owner had managed to escape. We wondered what had happened to the passengers and crew when the plane crashed. Back at the base I tried to find out but there were no details on record.

Seeing how much coral had grown around the plane's propeller made it clear to me why Navy personnel had been complaining for months about the boat channel on the south side of the island, claiming that the coral heads were scraping the bottom of their ships. Since the channel was supposed to be twenty feet deep they couldn't understand why they were scraping. Fisher and I decided to dive down and see what was wrong.

We swam out to the entrance of the channel and worked our way back. The trouble was quite obvious. Coral heads, sometimes forty feet wide, were growing up from the bottom to within ten or twelve feet of the surface. Since some of the Navy ships drew up to fifteen feet of water, it was no surprise they were scraping. Something had to be done about the coral before some vessel holed a hull.

When we reported our findings the Navy requested that the base take care of it and clear the channel. Fisher and I immediately volunteered for the job.

Surveying the area underwater we found eight huge coral heads that had to be blasted out. Most of them were along the sides of the channel but some were out in the middle. All around the coral heads was coral sand, which meant these formations had grown back in the few years since the original dredging. While Fisher and I were not demolition experts, we'd had some experience along that line. I had handled and used dynamite on a road job in Michigan, and more recently both Fisher and I had used explosives on the island. We blew up a barge that obstructed our bathing beach by using several one-pound TNT charges. The channel-clearing operation didn't appear to be much more difficult.

After conferring with the Navy and getting their go-ahead, I suggested to Colonel Bentley that we do the job ourselves using the C-3 plastic explosives, primercord and fuses that we already had on the island. An explosives expert named Mr. English, who was with the Corps of Engineers, volunteered his help. The three of us figured we could do the whole thing in about two weeks, thus saving the government the considerable expense of contracting the job to demolition people who would have to fly out from Honolulu.

When I explained our plan to Colonel Bentley he said, "I don't think it's a good idea, Major . . . too dangerous. Headquarters can send over more qualified people and it'll be out of our hands."

I told him we had an explosives expert with us and that we were qualified divers capable of handling the situation without bringing in outsiders. "Besides," I said, "the Navy's anxious to get it done. If we wait to go through channels it'll take two months just to start the paperwork."

Despite my argument the Colonel refused to budge on the subject. I don't know if he thought we'd blow ourselves to kingdom come or whether he was afraid all that commotion would attract sharks and we'd end up there that way. In either case it would amount to a lot of explanations and paperwork on his part. Much easier to let someone else have the responsibility. At least that's the way his reasoning seemed to us.

I felt we would have a better chance selling our idea to the upper echelon people in Hawaii.

I caught the next flight to Honolulu, went to headquarters and submitted our plan. The staff officers were all in favor of letting us do the job, especially since no funds would have to be budgeted for the project. When I told them how Colonel Bentley felt about it, the officer in charge said not to worry. He would send a directive to our C.O. asking him to enlist volunteers on the island to blow up the coral heads.

Without further ado the message was sent, and when we returned to Johnston the project had its volunteers. We were raring to go!

Assembling our equipment—explosives, primercord, fuses and several cans of TNT from supply—our project got under way.

First we motored out and selected a likely coral head. Fisher and I dove down to look it over. Back in the boat we held a conference on how we should do the job. We all came to the same conclusion—a wad of explosive, primercord and long fuse, the whole thing strategically placed. And boom! No coral head.

How simple it sounded. Wrapping the C–3 around a cap with a length of primercord attached, we put this in a burlap bag and planted it in the center of the coral head. The charge had a five-minute fuse.

Back in the boat we waited. Nothing happened. Five minutes passed. We gave it an extra five, then dove down to see what was wrong. The dynamite cap had exploded, but it lacked enough punch to fire off the C–3. We tried two more duds.

Concluding that the plastic explosive needed more of a shock in order to detonate, we put several one-pound cans of TNT in the center of the C–3. With a cap taped to the TNT and a five-minute fuse, we ignited the thing, retired about 300 feet from the scene and waited to see what would happen. We felt perfectly safe where we were.

Suddenly, with a muffled roar, part of the channel shot straight up into the air like a Polaris missile. We all stared, but Fisher and I jumped from one bare foot to the other, not so much from joy as from the sting of the concussion through the bottom of the boat. But we were jubilant too. The explosion was a beaut. It must have been heard by everyone on the island and ten miles out at sea.

After everything settled, I dove down to inspect the coral head.

It was still standing, a big hole blasted in its middle! "My God," I thought, "it's going to take several hundred pounds of explosive just for one coral head."

That night our demolition team was quite discouraged. It looked like we weren't going to be able to do the job after all.

The next morning we returned to the site. I went down to look at the coral head to see what we might be able to do differently.

There was nothing but broken coral everywhere! It was all over the place! Apparently the charge had completely shattered the coral head, but it took the heavy tidal currents to push the whole thing over and spread it across the bottom. My spirits rose considerably.

As soon as I popped out of the water I yelled, "Hey, you guys, we did it! We blew the blasted thing away yesterday. It just hadn't fallen over!"

Fisher and English were delighted. Once we knew our method was successful we were on our way. The only change we made was to move the boat another hundred feet farther away from the blast site to keep from raising blisters on the bottoms of our feet every time a charge went off.

Colonel Bentley was pleased with our success, but we were the only ones he allowed on the project. In the next couple of weeks our progress was periodically noted by those on shore whenever there was a muffled explosion and part of the channel shot up into the sky in a towering white geyser.

Attracted by the explosions and the possibilities of fresh-killed fish, the sharks homed in on our channel activities. They were there when we went down to look over a coral head and they were there when we checked the area after a blast . . . not always in the same condition, however. A few started coming close to us when we placed the charges so we took turns, one of us setting the explosives while the other butted away sharks.

After the fireworks, when we went down to inspect, the sharks were still there, stunned, along with dozens of fragmented moray eels that had been inside their coral condominium that we had just blown to bits.

One afternoon Fisher and I were diving in the channel while English remained in the boat ready to rig charges when we found another coral head that needed blasting. We carried our spearguns, just in case, but we had been in the water for a couple hours and hadn't seen a shark.

I began to think they were off somewhere having a convention when four jacks swam by and Fisher shot one weighing about six pounds.

Before the fish took the slack out of the spear cable, three small sharks appeared out of nowhere and tried to get the fish.

Seconds later they had help—several more showed up. Frantically the jack ricocheted around Fisher with the sharks racing close behind.

"Keep the fish away from them until I can shoot a shark," I shouted.

I dove down and fired at a 4 1/2-footer. When the spear only creased his back, I finned fast for the surface to reload. Meanwhile, Fisher pulled and jerked his spear cable to keep the zigzagging jack out of the jaws of the sharks. The fish was eager to oblige. He zipped this way and that, and for an instant Fisher looked like he was flying a fast Japanese fighter kite.

By the time I was reloaded ten sharks were chasing Fisher's slowly weakening silver kite. Suddenly, dooms-ville. A nine-footer swept in to engulf Fisher's fish, spear and all. The little sharks got out of his way fast lest they be next on his menu.

The big shark started to swim away. When he got to the end of Fisher's cable and felt a little restraint, he lurched, bending Fisher's spear at a ninety degree angle. Then the spear pulled from his mouth. Fisher hastened to reload with another spear, but by then it was too late. The sharks had vanished as fast as they had appeared.

After about nine days of blasting we had cleared the ship channel of coral heads. We had also stunned or decimated a sizable share of the local shark and moray eel population.

Not long after this I was swimming about 1000 feet out of the channel in an area I had never explored before on the south side of Sand Island. I was watching the bottom twenty-five feet below me, looking for something to spear. As my eyes moved over the sun-dappled marine landscape, they suddenly stopped on something that had no business being there.

Even with the marine growth on it I had no trouble recognizing the huge bomb that lay just beneath me. It looked like a thousand-pounder. I dove down and examined it carefully, not touching it. The detonating mechanism was completely corroded. I suspected that the bomb was from some World War II aircraft that had taken off from Johnston, developed engine trouble and had to jettison it in order to gain altitude to keep from crashing.

Back at the base I reported my find to Colonel Bentley and suggested that he let his "demolition team" take care of it. I said, "We can blow it up the same way we did the coral heads, Colonel. We'll just use a longer fuse so that we can get back to Sand Island before she blows."

We weren't absolutely sure the bomb was alive, but it seemed a good idea to get rid of it anyway.

The Colonel absolutely refused to let us do this job alone. "Coral heads are one thing but this bomb is entirely too big and too dangerous for your crew, Major," he told me. "Let the real demolition experts handle this one. Perhaps your men can assist if they wish."

He called Honolulu and they sent out two Navy lieutenants who were demolition experts. They went down with me to inspect the bomb and felt that it was indeed alive, that we shouldn't fool around with it but should handle the situation with extreme caution.

We conferred on the best way to take care of the matter and finally decided to use a big charge of C–3 placed beside the bomb as we had done with the coral heads, using primercord, caps and TNT.

This we did, adding a fifteen-minute fuse. We lit the fuse, then swam swiftly for the safety of some sand bunkers on Sand Island, something we could crawl behind. The bomb wasn't too far off the island and we weren't too sure what was going to happen.

The minutes dragged by. Abruptly the ocean erupted in a thunderous explosion. A wall of water at least six hundred feet geysered into the air, taking with it coral rocks, bomb fragments and probably a curious shark or two.

Yes, the bomb was live all right. The hole it blew in the bottom was fifteen feet deep. It made the coral look like the crater of a small volcano.

Blowing up the coral heads in the ship channel, I discovered a small cave in the side of the bedrock about fifteen feet underwater and extending back about six feet. The tide came through the channel from the north heading south, the water racing along at least six or seven knots an hour—too fast to swim against. The only way for us to dive to the cave was on a fast hit-and-run ride with the current.

The cave, whose ceiling sloped to a point on the south side, usually harbored two or three sharks. I don't know why they stayed down there, but they remained still on the bottom. Perhaps the cave provided a sheltered place where they could sleep and still have their gills aerated by the swiftly flowing current through the channel.

I had never seen this before, but in recent years divers have found large sharks lying motionless and apparently asleep in caves along the Yucatán coast. Most species of sharks must swim constantly to breathe. But some, such as the nurse shark *(Ginglymostoma cirratum)*, can remain motionless and pump water through their own gills. Others either have to swim continuously or rely on aerating ocean currents, as did the sharks I saw in the cave. Scientists are always interested in why sharks stay in these sometimes secluded places. In this instance, at least, I feel sure they were simply resting or sleeping.

If we dove down and disturbed them their first reaction was to bolt forward, wedging their snouts between the ceiling and floor, getting stuck there momentarily until they wriggled around and finally streaked out of the cave. It was always a bit awkward for a big shark sleeping with his head toward the wall when someone came up and tickled his tail, because sharks can't swim backward. Wall or no wall, they had to go forward.

In early 1954 several scientists came to the island in connection with atomic bomb tests that were to take place on Bikini Atoll over 1,500 miles away. One was the noted physicist Dr. Enrico Fermi, who received the Nobel Prize in Physics in 1938; later he helped develop the atomic bomb at Los Alamos.

Dr. Fermi talked to me about the underwater work we had done on the island. He was no diver or I would have taken him down. But he was most interested in the bottom contours and layout of the coral reefs around the island. As I realized later, this was all relative to preparation for the Bikini tests.

Accompanying Dr. Fermi was amiable James Stewart, diving officer for the Scripps Institute of Oceanography at La Jolla, California. Stewart and I became close friends.

He was an excellent diver who accompanied me on several trips to the reef and had no fear of our sharks. Unfortunately, Jim was destined to be involved in a bad shark attack off Wake Island on March 9, 1961. Stewart was diving with expert diver and professional underwater photographer Ron Church when it appeared that the two men accidentally blocked the path of a six-foot shark that was between them and the shore. At the time they thought the species was a blacktip. But from a photograph Church made just prior to the attack, and from the circumstances that followed, shark authorities later identified the species as *Carcharhinus menisorrah,* the gray reef shark common to these waters.

Anyway, the shark began turning its head back and forth and swimming in an erratic manner. The pectoral fins were held at an angle lower than usual, the shark's back was arched and its snout bowed up as it continued swinging its head in as wide an arc as the swing of its tail. Swimming swiftly it came in toward Stewart, passed him, then whirled and charged directly at his face. Stewart threw up his crooked right arm to fend off the shark and was bitten severely on his elbow—two quick bites before the shark let go. Church swam quickly between Stewart and the attacking shark and remained there until the attacker swam away. No one knows who or what irritated the shark to this degree. The divers were fortunate to have escaped with no more serious injuries.

Stewart and Dr. Fermi had come to Johnston Island to set up a special project. Since I was in charge of the diving on the island and knew something about the reefs, they asked me to help with the project. Neither of the scientists offered to fill me in on what it was all about, only that the operation had to be completed before the bomb blast. I was simply to follow instructions and would be told no more than I needed to know.

Eventually I learned that the project involved five small black boxes about a foot square designed and built by a California physicist. The boxes contained instruments for detecting underwater shock waves from the atomic tests that would take place on Bikini. They were to be installed at Johnston Island and other islands from 1,000 to 1,500 miles from the test site and often 3,000 miles apart. Very hush-hush. Project Black Box was top-secret stuff.

Surveying the reef to determine the best location for installing the box, I chose a spot in the lagoon near a deep channel leading out to open water. The black box with its recording device was to be affixed to a tripod that sat on the reef. Attached to the instrument in the box was a plastic hose that ran through the channel to a sensing device outside the reef that picked up the shock waves.

On the strength of my advice they built the tripod to support the black box at a height of about eight feet out of the water. This was to protect the recorder from occasional big wave action, which sometimes occurred when we had wind from the south. In my machine shop I had the tripod built of four-inch pipe to my specifications. Then I personally installed it, weighing down each leg with several hundred pounds of lead to make sure that any unusual wave action would not topple it.

Contrary to my advice, however, someone decided that eight feet was too high above water level and that a three-foot height would be adequate.

As the big day of the bomb blast approached, everything was ready. The scientists were standing by, the black box was on its tripod, the sensor was ready to pick up the shock waves. Then, the night before the big blast at Bikini, we got a south wind. The big ocean waves rolled in over the reef, and when they rolled out again, with them went the government's top-secret black box.

What a memorable time that was. We had blown the coral, we had blown the bomb, and now, with a little help, we had blown the government's Project Black Box.

I hope that the other black boxes scattered around the Pacific got more information than ours did.

7

~~~~~~ *meeting the man-eaters of antalya*

AS ALL GOOD things must, my tour of duty at the Johnston Island Air Force Base finally came to an end. After a brief stay at Biggs Air Force Base in El Paso, Texas, in the late fall of 1954, I got one of the biggest breaks in my Air Force career. A call came to the base from Washington, D.C., asking for a civil engineer to join the Mission Group in Turkey. Fifteen radar sites on the new NATO bases were being built there. I would be attached to the embassy staff and my job would be to advise my counterpart, a Turkish engineer on the Turkish general staff, about their construction. Since our group would be stationed in Ankara, it looked like I was in for a whole new adventure. As I left Massachusetts on my flight for Turkey that December, I wondered what kind of diving I would find there.

During the flight I became acquainted with two Turkish army officers, Major Binbasi Ali Resat Aktugan and Major Neriman Tamer, both of whom had been trained in the United States. In the course of our conversation we had long discussions about Turkey and my new tour of duty. I told them of my diving experiences with sharks off Johnston Island.

Major Aktugan listened intently, then slowly shook his head in disbelief. "You must be a very brave man to get in the water with those dangerous fish," he said. "I would not have the courage. But then, perhaps your sharks were not as dangerous as our Turkish sharks. Who knows?" He shrugged.

"Sharks in Turkey?" I asked. "It's funny but I never thought about them being there. But of course you have the Mediterranean."

"Certainly, my friend, why not?" he laughed. "We have many sharks—bad ones—what you call . . . man-eaters, no?" He glanced at Major Tamer for affirmation; his friend nodded.

"Let me tell you," said Aktugan. "I was born in Antalya on the Mediterranean. Our history goes back ten thousand years. You know Saint Nicholas, the one you call Santa Claus? Well, he was born there too, in my hometown, Antalya." He paused, grinning, waiting for an appropriate response from me.

I told him I bet all the Antalya kids were pleased about that.

"Yes, indeed," he smiled. "The city was once Greek. We have many antiquities, many old Greek temples and ruins thousands of years old. I suspect even the sharks came here thousands of years ago."

"Why there?" I asked. "What would attract them?"

"Blood, Major. Blood of the butchers."

When I frowned at that, Aktugan hastened to explain. "Behind our city are high mountains. For thousands of years the people who live on the cliffs above Antalya have always butchered their sheep beside a certain stream that flows over the cliffs into the sea. The blood and bits of flesh draw sharks there like flies to a dunghill. You should see the monsters fight over the sheep scraps," said Aktugan. "They are very ugly, very bad."

I said I could well imagine. I told him I had heard that blood attracted sharks but I thought wounded fish in the water acted as a stronger attraction.

"Perhaps," he shrugged. "I'm no diver, but I was raised in Antalya and many times from the high cliffs I have seen the sharks come to the bloody water at butchering time . . . so many sharks that the sea swarmed with them. And there were no wounded fish. Just the blood that brought them. All the people of Antalya know this. They fear the sharks. They never swim in the sea there because of them."

I told my two Turkish friends that during my stay in their country I hoped to have an opportunity to visit Antalya and to see for myself their dangerous sharks, perhaps even dive there. When I said that, I could tell by

Aktugan's slightly bemused smile that if I were foolish enough to try, surely it would be the last thing I ever did.

"Those sharks become kill crazy from the taste of that blood," he warned. "Never think of going into the water there if you value your life."

After I had been in Turkey for some time I became acquainted with an accomplished Turkish skin-diver, Edrdem Nayman, a young man about twenty-eight years old. I told him about meeting the Turkish officers on my flight over and what they had said about the sharks of Antalya. Then I asked if he would like to go there with me and try some diving.

"Gladly," he said, "but I'm not too sure about diving with those sharks. I'd just as soon keep all my parts together for diving another day," he laughed. "But I'll tell you what I'll do, Bill. I'll be glad to stand guard in the boat while you dive."

"Okay," I said, "that sounds fair enough."

We tossed my dive gear into a jeep and drove to Antalya over one of the most hellish roads imaginable, an obstacle course that had more ridges, ruts and rocks than smooth places. When we weren't dodging holes we were dodging flocks of sheep, whose herders scowled at us so disapprovingly I wondered if we had really missed the road and strayed off into one of their mountain grazing pastures.

But somehow we rattled and banged our way to Antalya. It looked just as ancient as Major Aktugan had described it. From all appearances it had indeed once been a large city in bygone times. But now it was a small village surrounded by the ruins of an ancient civilization obviously more prosperous than the present one.

We surveyed the area and finally determined where the farmers and herdsmen had been butchering their sheep for thousands of years. Climbing to the top of the cliffs and looking down on the sea below, we saw at least a dozen sharks cruising near the place where the mountain stream cascaded into the sea. It promised to be an exciting dive. Surely, in this remote area, the sharks had little opportunity to be disturbed by divers. I was curious to see how they would react to me. If what the Turkish officer said was true, I could expect some fast action from those silent shadows circling so serenely around the waterfall.

Nayman and I found a room at the local inn. The next morning we rented a boat and rowed to the place where the icy mountain stream fell into the Mediterranean. As I put on my mask and fins and slipped over the side into the water, Nayman assured me that he would steadfastly stand guard and keep a sharp lookout for me from the boat. The last thing I heard him call as I slid the spear down the barrel of my arbalete, stretched the rubbers and ducked underwater was, "In case they get you, Major, where do you want me to send the pieces?" That Nayman was a real Turkish delight.

Beneath the surface I headed for the waterfall. The closer I got the icier the water became. I surfaced for air and dove again. Then I saw it ahead of me, an interface in the saltwater sea, an area that looked like a wall of clear shimmering gelatin where the salt and fresh water mixed together.

As I dived down through this disturbed area the visibility soon cleared and I saw five sharks cruising languidly not far below me. The largest was about eight feet long. I looked at them and they looked at me, and paid me not the slightest attention.

Finally I had to surface for air. I snorkeled across the surface, following the shadows below. Selecting one, I quickly hyperventilated to load up with air, then dove swiftly toward him with the arbalete pointed and ready to fire.

But instead of showing some interest in my move by circling back toward me as a Johnston Island shark might have done, this one adroitly kept himself well out of my spearing range.

Thinking that perhaps he had had some previous bad experience with a diver and was abnormally skittish, I swam some distance away, selected another shark and surface-dived down to him.

Oddly enough this one also avoided me, swimming swiftly out of range. Indeed, for the next two hours while my fearful friend Nayman stood by anxiously in the boat expecting at any minute to see me torn to bits by the blood-thirsty Turkish sharks, I dove down repeatedly and tried to approach the sharks without success.

Finally, after being unable to get close enough to any of them to even fire my arbalete, I gave up. The sharks were not even remotely interested in my efforts. So much for Major Aktugan's bloodthirsty Turkish man-eaters. Maybe I just wasn't sheepish enough for them.

Next day as we bumped and gyrated our way home over the sheepherder's road, I wondered why the sharks had proved so shy. Had they been hunted before? Would they have reacted differently if I had acted afraid and tried to flee from them? Possibly so. Maybe they acted the way they did because I had stood my ground and in this case was actually the aggressor. I firmly believe that all animals, particularly the wild ones, can sense this attitude, and that it can change their idea about completing an attack.

An incident with half-tamed wolves a few weeks later seemed to bear this out. Our job in Turkey was made easier through the use of interpreters. Four of them worked in our office and one man in particular, Kemali Yenyalli, a graduate engineer of Iranian extraction who spoke fifteen languages and several dialects, often accompanied me as a translator on my trips afield. In fact, Kemali eventually became my son-in-law when he married my daughter Kathryn.

On one of our jobs together, Kemali and I with two Turkish engineers went up into the mountains to help plot a radar site. Our team made up a preliminary survey group figuring out the best ways to build main and access roads into the construction site near Smyrna, now Izmir. We drove our jeeps into the mountains as far as we could go, then got out and started hiking the last couple of miles into the radar site.

It was a clear, cool morning and the scenery was breathtaking. From the mountainous highlands we could see the whole harbor of Smyrna, a beautiful sight. The area we were in was very remote, inhabited only by Turkish sheepherders who were not overly enthusiastic about our invading their privacy and intruding on their grazing lands. Since wild wolves were a hazard to the flocks in this region, the sheepherders captured young wolves and trained them to protect the flocks. They put spiked collars around their guard wolves' necks to protect their throats from the wild wolves. These "sheepdogs" were fully as vicious as their wild brothers. They were only obedient to their masters, the sheepherders. Each shepherd had at least two of these guard wolves trained to attack anyone or anything that might approach the herd.

On this particular morning as we made our way along the trail toward the radar site, Kemali and the two Turkish engineers were about half a mile ahead of me. I was taking my time, walking slowly and enjoying the scenery, when I heard a commotion of barking and howling dogs some distance off. Then I saw the shepherd several hundred feet away. Racing toward me were his two half-wild wolves.

Realizing that I was in real danger, I stopped dead in my tracks, stood perfectly still with my hands across my chest in such a position that if the animals attacked my throat I could protect myself. I had no stick in my hand, but felt that these animals could be no more vicious than sharks.

The wolves charged toward me at high speed while I remained still. They came within four feet of me and suddenly stopped. We stared at each other and I thought, "Maybe I'll at least get out of this thing without losing an arm."

By then the shepherd, who was yelling at the wolves, ran over to where we were and dragged the growling, snarling beasts away. I'll never know what would have happened had he not arrived just then. But I feel sure that standing still and facing the wild animals, without showing fear, was what really saved me. Proof of this came about three weeks later when we made another trip to the site, accompanied by several Turkish and American generals.

Officers from the communications group who would be manning the site were also with us. Each U.S. officer was telling his Turkish counterpart how the site would operate when completed. As we approached the area, in the distance I saw this same shepherd with his wolves guarding his flock. One of the communications officers, who was carrying a walking stick, started back to the jeep to pick up some papers he had forgotten. As he crossed the field, leaving the rest of us standing around talking, I saw the two wolf dogs take off after him.

The shepherd shouted to them but it was too late. They were intent on attacking this lone intruder. Abruptly the colonel saw the wolves heading his way; then they reached him. Terrified, he swung his stick at them.

The animals attacked. One wolf lunged for his throat. Luckily he threw up his arm to ward off the attack. The wolf grabbed him by the arm and pulled him to the ground. Both animals savagely mauled him before the shepherd got to the officer and dragged them off him.

The man's arm was badly torn. The best we could do was administer first aid and have him driven immediately to the American hospital at Smyrna. After that, I couldn't help but think of my experience a few weeks earlier. Had I reacted similarly instead of quietly confronting my attackers, I might also have been a candidate for the hospital.

8

monster hunting

AFTER SEPARATION from active duty in January 1958, I stayed in the Air Force Reserve and retired to Venice, Florida, on the Gulf of Mexico. This was the area I had learned to love and remembered so well from my early experiences there in the 1930s. It was a perfect place for a diver. Inland, hidden in the nearby jungle-like vegetation, were many large freshwater springs and deep sinkholes that had never been thoroughly explored by divers. Many people had heard about these places, but since they were so difficult to reach, few if any had ever dived in them. Yet the challenge was there: the old curiosity to see what was in the bottom of those things. And now I had the time to find out.

The same was true of the area offshore. Here were some of the finest diving waters in the world, the clear, warm waters of the Gulf of Mexico where sharks, rays, tarpon and great schools of other fish constantly swam. Moreover, the Venice beaches were loaded with small black fossil shark teeth. Where had they come from, I wondered? What secrets lay buried beneath the white sand bottom a few hundred yards from shore? While I had yet to explore these places closely, from what I had seen there were enough exciting things to be discovered offshore to last a man several lifetimes.

Not long after I returned to Venice one of my first encounters some distance from the beach was with my old friend the shark. I was offshore about 600 feet, free diving for fossil shark teeth much to the amusement of my young son, Willy, whom I had taught to dive when he was four years old. On this particular day Willy was comfortably lying on an inner tube with his face mask and fins, watching me search the bottom below. As I dove to a rock pile about twenty-five feet down, I saw a large nurse shark lying apparently asleep under a rock arch. Two feet of his tail stuck out in my direction. Looking at this temptation, I wondered if I could possibly catch the shark by hand. If I could, what a show it would be for Willy, sitting up there in his ringside seat.

Surfacing quickly, I told him what I had seen and what I had in mind. His eyes widened behind his oversize face mask.

"Do you really think we could catch him, Daddy? A live shark?" he asked excitedly.

"Well, we'll certainly try, son. Let me see the rope I used to tow you out here."

Untying it from the inner tube, I put a noose in one end and coiled the rest. After hyperventilating, I dove back down to the bottom. With utmost care I eased up behind the shark. Since his head was under the rock arch he couldn't see me. Slowly I reached out, paused, then grabbed him just ahead of his caudal fin.

The instant he felt me he woke up with a bang. Only the arch prevented him breaking out into the wild blue yonder. Instead he shot forward, dragging me with him, whipping me back and forth with his powerful tail.

First he tried to drag me through the stone arch, but we were both too broad. Next we rolled and twisted in a cloud of mud, battering each other around for a good couple of minutes, with me trying to pull him out and him trying to pull me in. Finally, with neither of us winning the tug-of-war and my lungs about to burst, I slipped the noose over the shark's tail, jerked it snug and shot for the surface, holding tight to the other end of the rope.

Willy was beside himself, thoroughly enjoying his view of the show.

Grabbing a breath I dove again, following the line down to the shark, and we had another free-for-all. This time I managed to haul him out from under the stone arch and we went round and round in the water. When he tried to swim off I went along for the ride, until my weight stopped his run. When he turned and swam back toward me, I avoided him and managed to throw him off balance with a tug on the tail rope, to prevent him getting a bite of me.

Twice more I surfaced, then dove down to try to persuade him to let me lead him where I wanted. Finally the shark tired enough for Willy and me to start towing him in.

It was slow progress, with us holding on to the inner tube while swimming toward the beach 600 feet away, dragging the shark behind us. When the shark was headed in the same direction as we were I let up on the rope and he swam on his own. Once I looked down and saw he was directly below us.

Willy was as excited as any youngster could be who was at that moment leading home a very lively six-foot shark on the end of a twenty-five-foot leash. Long before we reached shore he yelled the news to the crowd of bystanders gathered on the beach wondering what was happening.

"Look! Look! My daddy's caught a big shark! He's got him right here!"

But before we got our catch ashore the big shark acted as if he had caught Daddy instead of the other way around. He bulldozed off a couple of times, taking me with him. Twice he pulled me underwater to the point where I figured if I couldn't get him back to the surface I was going to drown.

Finally, however, I worked him into the surf where I could touch bottom and do more with my reluctant captive. As we got closer to shore some of the anxious crowd splashed out and gave me a hand with the rope. Between us we hauled the thrashing shark the remaining few yards onto the beach.

The shark was quite a crowd-pleaser. No one quite believed that I had caught him by hand. But my beaming son Willy did, and that was all that mattered. Now I debated what to do with our catch.

Since the animal was quite unharmed, I wondered if Dr. Eugenie Clark, my friend at the Cape Haze Marine Laboratory at nearby Placida, would care to have it. I knew Genie was doing some shark research, so I gave her a call.

"Sure, Bill, we'd love to have it," she said over the phone. "Can you keep it alive until I send someone with the truck to pick it up?" I assured her that we could.

We slid the shark back into the water, keeping a firm grip on the rope while awaiting the truck from the lab.

I had met Genie Clark through mutual friends in Sarasota. She was a petite, darkly attractive young ichthyologist totally involved in learning all she could about the underwater world and its fascinating marine life. Having been trained as a diver while working at the Scripps Institute of Oceanography in California, she was quite skilled at it. Genie loved everything about the sport. The sea was her oyster and she was fast opening it. Not surprisingly, she was as adept with a dip net or handspear for collecting specimens as she was with the dissecting scalpel and microscope for studying them. On our first diving trip together we became fast friends.

We had both been invited to join a group heading offshore in their boat to look for sharks. We dove all day in the Gulf, checking out everything that came our way in the forty-foot-deep water. No sharks showed up, but I found a curious-looking sea hare and brought it up for Genie to identify. As luck would have it, the slimy purple-black blob turned out to be an extremely rare mollusk with the fancy latin name *Aplysia floridensis*. Since so few specimens of this unusual sea hare had ever been collected before, Genie was elated with my find. Later she wrote about the episode in her book, *The Lady and the Sharks.*

Since Genie is the daughter of an American father and a Japanese mother, she has always been fond of the Japanese delicacy, raw fish. On this particular trip while the other divers were on the boat resting between dives, I speared a ten-pound king mackerel with my Hawaiian sling and brought it aboard. Scaling the fish, I sliced off a small piece and began eating it raw. Amused by everyone's reaction, Genie joined me in the delicious repast. The other divers watched in disgust, thinking surely we both had very peculiar tastes.

Later Genie invited me to visit the laboratory she ran at Placida. When she explained the kind of research they were doing on the Gulf marine life, I was fascinated, especially by the work being done with sharks. Shortly afterward, a trip to the Florida Keys was planned and Genie asked if I would try an experiment on sharks while there. Of course I readily agreed.

Accompanying me on the trip was author and underwater photographer, William M. Stephens, then editor and publisher of *Underwater,* a diving magazine. This was to be a shark-fishing trip combined with a scientific experiment. Joined by Bill Stephens' young son, the three of us headed out from Key West in Bill's fine boat and dropped anchor off the Marquesas Keys, an uninhabited group of low-lying islands about thirty miles west of Key West.

While there we sampled a little of everything the underwater area had to offer. Bill caught sharks three to four feet long while wading and casting with lightweight fishing gear in the sand flats, and later took underwater photos of me harpooning a big barracuda. After photographing me spearing a six-foot moray eel we headed out toward the deeper water south of the Marquesas and got into the more serious job of catching larger sharks on heavier sportfishing tackle.

Anchoring the boat near a place where the bottom dropped off into the deeper water of the Gulf Stream, we baited with bloody slabs of bonito and waited for the action to begin.

After awhile the sharks picked up the savory trail of bonito blood and we were in business. Soon we had caught a number of lemon sharks ranging from four to six feet. Finally, after tiring a six-footer with the sharkfishing rig, Stephens suggested we try the experiment.

Genie had discovered two abdominal pores near the anus of sharks and was curious about the function of these apertures. She had said, "If you and Bill Stephens catch a good specimen, I want you to inject a colored dye into the shark's belly and then dive down with him in deep water to see if any dye is ejected through these pores while he is under pressure."

Since the lemon Stephens had caught was fairly docile after fighting the hook and line, he was no problem to handle. We injected the dye and I got into the water with him, wearing scuba. I also wore a shirt and pants as protection from the shark's rough hide.

Getting a good grip on the lemon, I swam him down through the gradually deepening water until I paused at 125 feet to examine him. As far as I could tell, no dye was coming out of the anal pores. After waiting at that depth a few moments to be absolutely certain, I started toward the surface. Halfway there, the shark became a lot more lively. Apparently our swimming had aerated his gills enough to snap him out of his lethargy.

In fact, he came out of it so well that I had trouble holding onto him. Straddling the shark with my legs around his middle and my hands gripping his pectoral fins, I went for a ride, steering him as best I could toward the surface.

When Stephens saw the shark shoot about two feet out of the water with me on his back, he shouted, "My God, that's great! Can you do it again?"

I steered the shark back down and came to the surface again not far from where Bill was leaning over the side of the boat snapping pictures with his camera.

I had forgotten the incident until March 1960 when I was surprised to see the whole episode written up by Stephens and published in an issue of *The Saturday Evening Post*. I walked down to the local drugstore to get a copy of the magazine. A stack of *Saturday Evening Posts* five feet high stood beside the cashier. Apparently they anticipated a big sale of the magazine with its story of the local kook who rode sharks.

As I bought a copy, someone recognized me. Pointing me out he said in a loud voice, "Hey, there's that crazy guy who rides sharks!" The other people in the store sort of jumped back as if I had leprosy. Maybe they thought whatever it was that made me do such a reckless, irrational thing was contagious. I'd never really thought about it before, but it was an odd kind of infamy. Tucking the magazine under my arm, I ducked my head and hurried home before anyone else recognized me.

In the next few months a series of adventures and misadventures took me off to Texas and then to Cuba on more shark-diving trips. Whether we were just unlucky or what I'll never know, but we found the Cuban sharks to be just about as cooperative as the Turkish "man-eaters" of Antalya. We were simply unable to approach them.

It was some time before I returned to Venice again. But soon after I was back I visited the Cape Haze Marine Laboratory, which had moved from Placida to near Sarasota on the southern tip of Siesta Key, a place called Midnight Pass.

Eugenie Clark's shark research had escalated considerably. Now other scientists were coming from various parts of the United States to study the animals for their own research projects. Consequently, Genie was requiring a lot more live sharks. Capturing them in good condition and keeping them that way was a problem she had right from the beginning of her tenure as director of the laboratory. And it had not improved much.

In their natural environment sharks are tough, healthy, practically indestructible animals. But getting them from this ocean environment and transferring them to the shark pens at the laboratory without harming them was a more delicate operation than anyone would believe.

Genie was catching sharks with a commercial fishing rig called a Japanese long-line. This was a 300-foot length of three-quarter inch manila rope anchored at both ends and containing sixteen spliced loops spaced sixteen feet apart. From these loops hung dropper lines attached with modified quick-release becket knots. Each dropper line was a six-foot length of manila spliced to a three-foot chain that held a large 2 1/2-inch shark hook. Flagged buoys on twenty-foot ropes marked the ends of the long-line. Right from the beginning Genie caught many sharks on this rig. But each morning when she checked the line, only a few were still alive. And towing these back to the laboratory from almost three miles at sea often drowned them. Nor could the huge animals tolerate being lifted aboard her catch boat. What few people realized was that although sharks out of water may weigh several hundred pounds, in the water their actual water-buoyed weight may be no more than seven or eight pounds, a phenomenon caused in part by the shark's enormous liver, the oil of which is lighter than water; therefore the organ serves as a kind of ballast tank.

When Genie and her assistants tried to hoist these large animals tail-first into the boat, the sharks lost the support of the water and the animal's internal organs were crushed by their own weight.

Genie's shark-catching team finally solved the problem by building a big live-tank in the catch boat's cockpit, where the sharks were placed with a minimum of lifting. They were then hustled back to the laboratory and put in a holding pen. This method proved quite successful, for most of the sharks arrived in far better condition than before.

Once inside the holding pen some of the newly captured specimens still often acted more dead than alive, sinking to the bottom and refusing to swim. Handlers would then get into the shallow end of the pool and "walk" the animal around the enclosure, circulating water through the shark's gills until he eventually revived.

As effective as this method was for catching sharks, Genie constantly needed more. When I visited the laboratory the current fishing captain was having difficulty supplying enough sharks for her needs. Although he was an experienced Nova Scotia commercial fisherman, I wasn't too sure how knowledgeable he was about catching sharks. Genie wondered aloud to me if I might be able to help with the problem.

"Bill," she said, "I'd appreciate it if you'd go out with the captain and give him a hand. We can use just as many sharks as we can get, so any suggestion you might have for speeding up the operation would be a big help."

I told her I would be glad to do whatever I could. Genie introduced me to the boat captain and asked if he minded my going along to help him. She told him I had had considerable experience with sharks all over the world and that I might be instrumental in increasing the numbers of sharks taken.

Of course the man could not very well refuse, but I learned later that he was really quite angry to think that she had asked me to join him. On the way out in the catch boat he proved to be an ill-tempered type. "Dammit," he said, "I'm captain of this boat and I'll take care of catching the sharks. Rigging those lines is my job and I'll do it just the way I want. You can help if you like, but don't forget who's in charge here. And don't try to interfere with anything I do."

I got the message. Genie had told me earlier that the captain was bringing in about one shark a day when they

really needed at least eight a day for their present research program. As far as I was concerned the situation
looked pretty hopeless with this arrogant character in
charge of the catch operation. But I went along with him
for a couple of days to see how he handled the situation.
One thing I soon realized that he handled very well was
several half-filled bottles of booze that he kept stashed in
various places around his boat. In the course of a day's
trip he managed to hit all of them; in fact, his score with
the bottles was far better than with the sharks. Half the
time he didn't even bother putting bait on the lines.
Since we were working two long-lines that were 300 feet
apiece, we should have been bringing in at least ten
sharks a day. But at the rate we were going we were lucky
to bring in one or two a day.

On the third day I showed up to work with him I found
he had declared a vacation and taken the day off. I was
there early that morning. Genie and several scientists
involved in shark liver research were standing around
wondering what to do.

Genie said, "Bill, would you please take out the boat
and find us some sharks?"

I said,"What about the captain? He told me in no
uncertain terms that he was in charge of the operation
and wanted no interference."

Genie confided that they were not at all satisfied with
the captain's catch record. She wanted me to go out and
see what kind of record I could make. I told her I would
give it a try.

I gassed up the *Rhincodon* and headed out to sea to see
what I could do. Instead of working close inshore as the
captain had been doing, I moved the two sets of long-

lines out into deeper water and baited them.

Several sharks hit the baits within a short time. Releasing the dropper lines from the main line, I eased the sharks into the holding tank on the stern of the boat. Some were up to ten feet long, making it necessary for their tails to hang out beyond the stern of the *Rhincodon.*

When I came in everyone was pleased to see how many sharks I'd caught, especially the visiting scientists who were now able to continue their experiments.

Genie asked me what I had done differently from what the captain was doing. All I could tell her was that I had gone out a bit farther and had sat there waiting for the sharks to hit.

The next morning when the captain arrived for work, Genie told him that from then on I was to be in charge of the catch operation, and if he wished to continue working for the laboratory, he was to take orders from me.

This was apparently more than the captain wanted to put up with. After collecting his half-filled booze bottles from the *Rhincodon,* that was the last we saw of him.

From then on I started using three long-lines and instead of going out two or three miles offshore, I went out eight to ten miles where the water was deeper and I felt there were more and larger sharks. A helper and I set the lines one day and motored out to check them the next. Our score for sharks that first day totaled fifteen, so many that we had a regular shark shuttle going between the long-lines and the laboratory in an effort to keep the animals alive.

Once I got into the swing of the job I really enjoyed it. I got in the habit of carrying my scuba gear with me so I could undertake some shark observations of my own. Frequently when we reached the marker buoys on our shark lines the next morning I would slip on a tank and go down to check out the catch to see how many were still alive. All told we were catching a good variety—at least three different species of hammerheads, two species of blacktips and the rest tigers, nurses, duskies, bulls, lemons and an occasional sandbar shark. In size they ranged from five to eleven feet long, with some hammerheads over fourteen feet.

Catching sharks had its hairy moments, but getting them back to the laboratory alive was the most difficult part. It was essential to the scientists that they arrive alive.

The holding tank in the stern of the *Rhincodon* was only eight feet long. A rear gate could be let down so we could guide in the sharks without having to lift them far out of water. If a shark was longer than the tank, we left the gate down so that his tail stuck out. The rest of him we secured in such a way that water would wash over his gills. Not an ideal setup, but it worked most of the time.

On one trip out I had trouble finding the marker buoy. The float was under the surface and only its flag showed above water. I knew something unusually large must be on the line to have pulled the float that far under. The bottom was about forty-five feet down. It was rough and uneven, with lots of limestone formations, some of them ten or fifteen feet high in places.

Putting on my scuba gear I went over the side to see what we had. Following the shark line down, I discovered that it led into a large underwater cavern. Inside was one of the biggest tiger sharks I had ever seen. He was over twelve feet long and he had to weigh well over 1,000 pounds. He was completely wrapped up in the line, all 300 feet of it. His gills were working; he was still alive.

As I looked at him hanging there I thought, "What a waste to let him die." I wondered if there was anything I could do to save him. Methodically I started unwrapping the rope from around his huge body, pulling and tugging the tight coils from his belly. The hook was still in his mouth. Once I got the line untangled I slowly worked him out of the cave into open water.

Gradually he began to move more energetically. So did I. I had no intention of hanging around with him until he got to feeling real good. It appeared that the tiger was going to survive after all.

With my helper's assistance we eased him into the holding tank and secured him. This was our only catch for the day since he had managed to drag the anchor and entangle himself in the whole rig—you might say he took it hook, line and sinker.

We stretched out the line again and rebaited the hooks. Then we took our prize shark back to the lab. The next day he was very much alive and swimming vigorously around the shark pen.

Later I learned that the liver alone of this particular shark weighed several hundred pounds.

On another offshore trip, with a visiting marine biologist, I found that both markers on one of the lines were underwater, barely touching the surface. Although I used dead reckoning in finding my sets, I could usually get within a few hundred feet of them. This time we were about ten miles out, and when I saw the buoys submerged I knew that once again we had big game.

Putting on the scuba gear, I went down to see what it was. I found several sharks on the line, but to my amazement my main catch was a huge sea turtle weighing 500 or 600 pounds. I had never seen one like it. My marine biologist friend was quite excited by the catch. We spent considerable time trying to get the turtle on board, but he proved too heavy for us to handle. So we pulled him up onto the platform on the stern, then tied him on with several wraps around both the turtle and the platform.

While we were securing the catch I failed to notice that the weather was blowing up a storm. Before we even started the waves were washing over the turtle and filling the boat. I had to do something quickly before we sank. If I couldn't get the engine started before we went under we would be in serious trouble. We already had a foot of water in the hold.

"Better put on your life vest just in case," I told my companions. I cut loose the shark line to avoid having to pull it in, got the engine running and started the bilge pump. Then we got underway.

The water stopped pouring in. Our real trouble, of course, was the weight of the turtle on the stern, but I hated to cut him loose because he would be a real prize back at the lab.

After the first few miles most of the water had been pumped out of the bilge and the situation was under control again.

Back at the lab Genie and the others were surprised to see our catch. They filmed us bringing the turtle from the *Rhincodon* into the shark pen, where he was kept for a few days of observation. Then we loaded him back into the boat, returned him to the Gulf and released him.

Before doing so, however, Genie drilled a small hole in his shell and attached a tag with a stainless steel wire. The tag requested anyone finding the turtle to please report it to the lab. To the best of my knowledge, nothing more has ever been heard of the turtle. Since these animals often live for over 100 years, it would be interesting if someone in the year 2060 called the laboratory to report finding our tagged turtle.

None of us would even be around to remember it!

9

~~~~~~~~~~~~~~~ *sharks for science*

WHAT WAS happening to all the sharks we were bringing in to the Cape Haze Laboratory? Why were so many needed? What were the scientists doing? Waging war against sharks and carrying on a calculated plan of shark eradication?

Not in the least. To better understand what was happening there, one needs to know a little about the background of this unique laboratory and the young woman who pioneered it, Eugenie Clark.

After extensive research on tropical fish at the American Museum of Natural History for her Ph.D., Eugenie's specialized knowledge in this field made her a logical choice of the Office of Naval Research for a one-person mission to the Pacific to study poisonous fishes.

After eighteen months on this project she returned to New York to receive her Ph.D. as an ichthyologist from New York University. A Fulbright Scholarship then took her to the Red Sea for a year. When she returned, Eugenie wrote of her adventures in *Lady with a Spear,* which in turn attracted the attention of Alfred and William Vanderbilt, who were interested in establishing a marine laboratory on Florida's Gulf Coast. When they offered Eugenie directorship of the lab, she accepted. In 1955, with little more than a boat, a wooden building for an office and an enormous amount of enthusiasm, she helped found the Cape Haze Marine Laboratory at Placida, Florida (now the Mote Marine Laboratory on Siesta Key, near Sarasota).

In the years that followed, the facility expanded and attracted scientists from all over the country with its potential for marine research. The various programs of research were assisted largely by support from the National Science Foundation, Office of Naval Research and the William and Marie Selby Foundation.

In the formative years one of the scientists who contacted Genie about working at the laboratory was Dr. John H. Heller, Director of the New England Institute for Medical Research. He had telephoned Genie from the "shark-infested" Caribbean where he was trying to get shark livers for his research, but he couldn't find any sharks.

"Would you people be able to catch me any sharks?" he asked.

Genie answered affirmatively, for she was already in-volved in her own study of sharks, particularly in trying to learn the function of the abdominal pores commonly found in sharks and other primitive fishes. From that point on, almost before she had settled in her laboratory, she found herself in the shark-hunting business on a large-scale basis.

Not long afterwards, Dr. Heller and his wife, Terry, came to Placida and involved themselves in the labora-tory's initial trials and tribulations of capturing big sharks on long-lines.

Initially, Dr. Heller was involved in research that sought to study cholesterol in the bloodstream, trying to learn why this fatty substance sometimes clogged arter-ies and caused coronary thrombosis. As one of the na-tion's outstanding research scientists in organic chemis-try, Dr. Heller hoped to tag cholesterol with a radioactive substance that would enable him to learn what caused a buildup of this material in the circulatory systems of his laboratory test animals.

The substance best suited for this type of tagging, he found, was squalene, identified by a biochemist as one of the fatty substances in the livers of giant basking sharks. But to make this substance into a tracer, radioactive car-bon had to be injected into live sharks. Since basking sharks attain a length of forty feet and weigh several tons, they were most unlikely laboratory animals. Dr. Heller searched elsewhere for smaller sharks. Having little luck finding them in the Caribbean, he appealed to Dr. Euge-nie Clark.

Small sharks also made squalene in their large livers—which sometimes comprised one seventh of the animal's body weight—but the amount was small. The test sharks

Dr. Heller got off the long-lines were injected with radio-active carbon, in the hope that they would produce carbon-tagged squalene, providing the sharks could be kept alive for a week or so. They were then put to death, their livers removed and processed for the radioactive substance.

Eventually Dr. Heller found that the sharks he had to deal with provided insufficient amounts of squalene, so, for then, the program was shelved.

Pursuing other avenues of research, Dr. Heller found an organic property in shark liver oil that stimulated the defense system of a laboratory test animal's body to work against infectious diseases. This started him thinking about a new approach to the prevention or cure of cancer, different from the cancer research programs in progress.

Dr. Heller reasoned that instead of looking simply for a specific agent that could be used to combat a specific form of cancer, why not employ a substance that would stimulate the body's defense mechanism to resist all kinds of cancer?

"The remarkable thing about cancer," said Dr. Heller, "is not that so many people get it, but that so many people do not because of an innate bodily resistance."

Scientists believe that several things cause cancer: chemicals, possibly viruses and radiations such as X rays. Dr. Heller estimated that annually an individual is exposed to anywhere from one to ten thousand malignant events from a single possible source of cancer. This is why he thought it remarkable that cancer is not more frequent than it is. "One can assume," he said, "that some mechanism defends the body against such malignant cells."

In subsequent research at the New England Institute, Dr. Heller found that in cancer-induced tumors in his research animals—tumors that were ordinarily 100 percent fatal—the animal was able to throw off the cancer completely in 40 to 60 percent of the cases when treated with lipide from shark livers. "This," he wrote, "means an absolute and permanent disappearance of a malignancy up to an inch in diameter."

Then problems arose as to what was the best dosage.

In the laboratory Dr. Heller and his assistants set about analyzing, separating and purifying the shark liver lipides so that they could isolate the beneficial material they wanted, analyze it and then synthesize it. But since sharks possessed an extraordinary number of lipides in their livers, this process was long and time-consuming. It would be impossible to know what dose of the active material they were giving until they had it isolated and pure.

As the doctor's research continued, it became obvious that he needed a greater supply of shark liver oil. The best source, he found, was in the lemon shark, an animal quite sensitive to temperature changes. In the early summer months lemons were commonly found off the Florida coast, but as the water temperature dropped later in the year, they retreated to the warmer Bahamas and Caribbean. In order to procure these sharks in the winter months, he had to go to the Bahamas. By careful study of the bottom topography, currents, reefs, shoals and water depths, he was able to accurately predict the best sites to find the sharks.

Once the lemons were caught and brought in alive, their livers were removed, quick-frozen, packed in dry ice in specially designed deep insulated cartons. A technician flew them back to New England with an adequate supply of dry ice so that the liver was maintained at a constant temperature of $-80°$ C.

Working out of the Lerner Marine Laboratory on Bimini in the Bahamas, and using the best equipped marine biological vessels, scientists had tried for three consecutive weeks to catch lemon sharks. They had found none. When Dr. Heller and two others arrived from the New England Institute for a week's stay, only one lemon was caught. Subsequent efforts in the Caribbean also failed. After that, Dr. Heller concentrated his shark-catching efforts in the Gulf of Mexico with the cooperation of Dr. Eugenie Clark and her Cape Haze facilities.

Sometime later, chemists from the Dow Chemical Company became interested in the New England Institute's research and sent a team of their top scientists to talk with Dr. Heller.

Excited over what Dr. Heller and his staff were doing, the Dow Chemical Company subsequently made available to him their organic analytic chemical section to help solve the problem of isolating and synthesizing the mysterious ingredient in shark liver lipide.

Consequently, Dr. Heller returned to the Cape Haze Laboratory with a small army of technicians and an ingenious super-miniaturized processing plant so designed that when freshly caught shark liver was put in one end, within a few hours purified lipide came out the other end! This one machine was capable of doing in a few hours what had taken three people three weeks to accomplish!

The next thing was to procure as much shark liver

lipide as possible by catching as many sharks as they could. By 1964 the Cape Haze facility was running as high as five shark lines with 150 hooks on them. These were baited, set and pulled twice a day, using about 450 pounds of one- to two-pound fish daily as bait. That many hooks were required because fish and crabs often stole the bait, as did species of sharks other than the lemons that were needed.

As soon as the sharks were caught they were brought into the holding pens, where the hooks were removed. If the shark seemed able to survive it would be kept in the pen alive. If it was not expected to live it was dispatched with a blow on the head with a sledgehammer in the shallow end of the pool and its huge livers were quickly dissected out. The remaining carcass was measured and examined by other marine biologists anxious to accumulate a variety of other information about sharks.

The shark liver was then quickly carried to the miniplant, which was set up under a huge tent on the grounds beside the laboratory. The fatty lobes of the liver were placed in a specially-built homogenizer designed to macerate it in sixty seconds so that the largest particle was smaller than a red blood cell. This was necessary to release the lipide from the cells. The macerating process was done in a large container in the presence of absolute alcohol and ether along with large chunks of dry ice. This reduced the temperature of the mixture to $-80°$ C. to preserve the active material the scientists wanted to extract from the liver.

The macerated liver was then processed by the miniplant and the end result was purified lipide.

Dr. Heller and his team then hoped to be able to find the active ingredients in this lipide, identify them and proceed toward their synthesis. The next step would be to see if this final substance would have the same beneficial results of stimulating the defense system in human bloodstreams to fight against and resist cancer, as it had in his laboratory research animals.

While Dr. Heller, his technicians and the mini-plant were operational at the laboratory the demand for sharks was always greatest. But not always did we recover all the sharks that got on our lines. Some escaped. And those that did I would like to have seen.

On two trips out I found my lines completely tangled up and only one flag-marker showing. There were several small sharks on the line, but a couple of the shark hooks were completely straightened out. In the past such a hook had been capable of holding a hammerhead shark over fourteen feet long. Something bigger and more powerful must have straightened out those hooks. I suspected that it was *Carcharodon carcharias,* the great white shark. While this species was not common to our area of the Gulf, I believed he was the culprit.

After that we wrote all the major hook manufacturers in the country trying to find a better product, but without success. I suggested that we contact an Australian firm, and after a long wait we learned that they made huge tempered steel shark hooks practically guaranteed to catch anything in the oceans.

Sometime after I left the job with the lab, Genie wrote that I was right. After using the Australian shark hooks, one of the set lines caught two great white sharks that weighed almost 1,000 pounds apiece!

As we came to the end of the summer season, Dr. Heller and his team returned to New England and our shark liver program slowed down. There was less need for the large number of sharks we had been bringing in daily. But one of the visiting scientists at the laboratory, Dr. Frederick Sudak from the Albert Einstein College of Medicine, Yeshiva University, New York City, asked me to take him down to the Florida Keys to catch nurse sharks, which he needed in cancer research experiments he was undertaking.

Since Dr. Sudak did not want the sharks injured in any way, I volunteered to dive and catch them by hand instead of with hook and line.

With a small crew to help us, we went to the Keys in the *Rhincodon* and began searching the bays and inshore waters along the Gulf side looking for sharks. We would anchor the boat in a likely area while I snorkeled around examining all the small caves in the limestone bottom until I found a sleeping shark. Then it was just a matter of grabbing him by the tail, dragging him out into the open and hanging on. Since the doctor was not much of a diver, I had most of this to do myself. Before long I had caught half a dozen nurse sharks ranging in size from 4 to 5 1/2 feet. We kept them in the large saltwater tank in the *Rhincodon* until they could be trucked back to the lab in a saltwater tank.

On our last day we switched our operation to the Atlantic and the grass beds. Here the water was only about six or eight feet deep over broad grass flats. Catching nurse sharks in the grass was not as easy as corraling them in the caves. When I saw one, I had to approach even more stealthily than before or he would see me and charge off in a cloud of silt before I could even get my hands on him. Many got away.

Those I caught I simply had to keep from reaching back and nipping me. Fortunately, nurse sharks do not have long teeth. But they do have powerful jaws, and once they take hold of something you practically have to kill them to get them to release it.

On the last day I saw in the distance a fifty-five-gallon oil drum on the bottom. Both ends were out, and inside the drum rested a nurse shark about 6 1/2 feet long. I figured this fellow would be too big and too heavy for me to handle, but I decided to take a crack at him anyway.

Swimming up very slowly behind him I brought my hands together and clamped them on his tail. You can imagine the commotion he made on the inside of that fifty-five-gallon drum. Underwater it sounded like a boilermaking factory. It was all I could do to keep him from going out the other side and pulling me right through the barrel. But I hung on for dear life, and gradually he tired enough for me to pull him out of the drum and work him over toward the boat, which was fifty feet away.

When I got alongside the *Rhincodon* I yelled for the crew to get a rope around the shark's body and to help me hoist him in. Understandably, they were not too eager to get near the shark's jaws. But one of the men grabbed his pectoral fins and helped lift him.

While we were all involved with trying to get him out of the water and into the boat, the shark reached down and bit my leg. His teeth didn't penetrate my flesh, but he held my trousers in a vicelike grip.

As the crew lifted the shark into the boat he still clung to my pants. Consequently, part of me came into the boat feet-first while the rest of me was underwater, where I was about to drown.

Somehow I got my head out and sputtered, "For God's sake, somebody get a knife and cut my pants off so I can get loose!"

I don't know if they were afraid to get near the shark's jaws after seeing what he was doing to me or whether they were afraid they would cut my leg off. They were no help whatsoever. Finally, in desperation, I managed to wriggle myself up backwards over the side of the boat and amputated my pant leg myself, freeing me from the shark's jaws. This was the one and only time I have ever been bitten by a shark. And this species happens to be one of the more peaceful members of the tribe. But let no one doubt that this innocent-looking, inadequately toothed nurse shark possesses all the spitfire tenaciousness of a bulldog once his ire is up.

The trip ended successfully with a number of fine unharmed nurse sharks delivered back to the lab ready for Dr. Sudak's cancer research. What I did not realize until his death several months later was that young Dr. Sudak, who was working desperately in his experiments with nurse sharks to find some substance that would at least arrest, if not cure, the progress of cancer, at the time himself had leukemia.

I continued catching sharks on the *Rhincodon* off Sarasota but only set out one shark line a day since the project was winding down and there was increasingly less need for sharks. Word got back to the lab's business manager that I had been diving on the shark lines. Since he didn't dive himself it was difficult for him to believe that someone would do anything as foolish as this.

Checking with our employees' insurance policy, he found that this aspect of my job was not covered. I was told to cease this nonsense immediately.

This took a lot of fun out of the job. Still, I knew such rules had to be obeyed. To make matters worse, shark-catching activities were almost at a standstill. So I terminated my job at the lab and decided to try the diving elsewhere.

10
～～～～～～ four-fathom fossils

NOW THAT I had more free time there were two areas I wanted to dive in and check out more closely: the Gulf bottom off Florida's Venice Beach and the so-called lost springs and sinkholes farther inland.

The beach at Venice was different from any beach I had ever seen or heard about. In some areas, near the water, the normally light-colored sand changed from amber to gray and finally to black, almost as black as some of the volcanic sand I had seen in the Hawaiian Islands.

The Venice Beach black sand was not volcanic, however. It was something else, but nothing I could identify
at first. Then I noticed that every weekend, and often
many times during the week, people walking along this
strand of beach usually stopped to pick up things from
the sand.

At first I thought they were the usual shell collectors
you saw along all the beaches in Florida. But when I went
up to see what they were doing, I found them collecting
something far more unique than seashells. They were
finding tiny black triangles—fossil shark teeth ranging in
size from a quarter of an inch up to an occasional tooth
an inch long. And the more I studied that black sand, the
more I realized that its color actually came from fossils
ground to bits by the tumbling action of the waves on the
quartz-silica shingle of sand at the water's edge. Merely
by watching that narrow strip one was rewarded by several tiny teeth that might appear with one wash of a wave
and disappear under the shifting sand and gravel with
the next, only to reappear with a third swish of water.

Talk about your dedicated collectors. Late one afternoon I counted twenty-three people of all ages who were
concentrating their efforts around a kind of natural rock
jetty that extended out into the Gulf for a few yards. For
some reason it seemed that the people were having better luck finding teeth around this natural formation than
other areas of the open beach. In any event they were
sharing a common experience and really enjoying themselves.

Their collecting equipment ranged from nothing
more elaborate than a plastic foam soft-drink cup or a
piece of hardware cloth to a perforated pie pan, a

French-fry strainer or the most deluxe of devices: a long-handled, screen-covered scoop sold locally for dredging up a crustacean fishbait at the edge of the surf. But whether they wielded a cup or a strainer, no one was shy about showing off their technique, a procedure that was simplicity itself. All the shark-tooth sleuths had to do was wade out a few feet into the water, scoop up the bottom in their strainers and bring the "ore" ashore for careful searching out of the small ebony nuggets. Some people simply dumped the material on the beach and spread it out with their hands while fingering the conglomeration of sand, gravel and broken shell. Others were more dainty, carefully spreading their scoopfuls out on large white terrycloth towels where even the poorest sighted of them would not miss spotting a black triangle against the white towel. The terrycloth crowd was mainly white-haired ladies with big straw hats and small leashed dogs, or pairs of maiden-lady schoolteachers with top-knotted hairdos and Calamine-coated noses.

Free-roaming collectors hurried in and out of the surf sorting almost in midstride, in contrast to more sedentary collectors on folding chairs at the water's edge who sifted and searched in comfort. Singling out one such rosy-cheeked gentleman in tee shirt and flowered shorts, I asked, "How many teeth do you usually find?"

He was prodding the gravel in his perforated pie pan with a pencil, using it like a chopstick, with his face close to the pan as if at any moment he might consume the works. Without looking up he said, " 'Bout twenty a bucketful."

"Any size?"

"Regular."

A flick of his wrist shot the gravel over his shoulder. Scooping another panful from a bucket near his knee, he tilted the bottom half of a bleach jug my way so I could see a double handful of the ebony triangles.

"Pretty good. What're you going to do with them?"

"Give 'm 'way."

"Well, good luck."

Leaving the talkative type I approached another, a gentleman from Illinois. Like the first man, he planned to give his teeth away.

"Last year I must have carted 600 teeth home with me," he said. "I gave them all away. But it wasn't enough. Other people heard about it and they wanted some. I guess this time when I go home I better be carrying about 1,000 of them with me."

An elderly lady sitting on a large beach towel methodically sorting through the pile of shell and gravel her husband had scooped out of the surf for her said, "I make mine into jewelry. Most of my friends make things from seashells, but I like to work with shark teeth. They're different. Do you know that my husband and I picked up our first tooth on this beach fifty years ago? Where in the world do you suppose they all come from?"

I wondered the same thing. Were they working up out of the sand and gravel at the edge of the beach, or were they all over the bottom offshore? The day Willy and I found the nurse shark, I was searching offshore for fossil teeth. But that wasn't my first trip.

On my first trip I had waited weeks for the water conditions to get good enough for me to see something on the bottom. Every time I came to the beach ready to dive, the water would look good from a distance. But when I checked it out closer, the water was often so milky I hardly had twelve inches of visibility.

Finally the right day came and I realized later we were enjoying a Bermuda high—a high-pressure area that hovered over Bermuda causing a clockwise weather pattern in our area. This brought a moderate east wind that moved clear water into our beaches. Strapping on a double-tank scuba rig, I swam out from the beach.

Close to shore was a buildup of cochina and loose debris constantly in a slurry of agitation from the waves. Beyond it the bottom was primarily light sand with patches of accumulated loose algal growth or grass washing in from deeper water. Some distance from shore, in about twelve feet of water, I occasionally saw bottom areas where either eddying currents or the scouring effect of the rolling surf had caused small concentrations of shells, gravel and small black shark teeth.

Whenever I paused in these places to fan the bottom I found teeth scattered in such numbers that a person could easily recover hundreds. But I was interested in finding big teeth. I had long believed that if the small teeth were there in such concentrations, surely there would also be larger ones—teeth five or six inches long that once belonged to *Carcharodon megalodon,* the nearly one-hundred-foot prehistoric ancestor of our present-day great white shark, *Carcharodon carcharias.*

I had once seen an old photograph of a reconstruction of *megalodon's* jaws in New York's American Museum of Natural History. Six mustachioed men were shown standing in the jaws surrounded by huge hand-size fossil shark teeth—hundreds of them. The caption beneath the photograph said the shark would have been about eighty feet long. Scientists believe that this giant animal once roamed Miocene seas from twelve million to twenty-six million years ago.

Reading more on the subject, I found that this shark might be one of the medium-size members of the species because bigger teeth than that were said to have been found in a place called Sharktooth Hill near Bakersfield, California, a long way from the ocean. When seventeenth-century naturalists first found these teeth they classified them as "fossil birds' tongues" or "vipers' teeth," for no one could even conceive of a shark the size of *megalodon*. Even today the largest tooth from the modern man-eater, *Carcharodon carcharias*, would measure less than two inches long. So the prehistoric forebear of the great white shark, with a jawful of several hundred teeth five to seven inches long, must have been a real terror.

While most authorities believe that *megalodon* is extinct today, a few are not so sure. Off the record they admit to the possibility that in some dark corner of the abyss, one or more giant carry-overs of *megalodon* may still roam the eternal darkness of the deep. This feeling gained support a number of years ago when the prehistoric coelacanth fish, thought extinct since the middle Mesozoic era 155 million years ago, was hauled up from the deep off Africa in the recent twentieth century, very much alive and kicking. In the years that followed, other coelacanths were caught. And interestingly, one of the curious clues that keeps alive some scientists' belief that *megalodon* might still exist is the fact that early in this century four-inch *Carcharodon megalodon* teeth were dredged up from the bed of the Pacific Ocean, and observers said the teeth seemed "fresh" rather than fossilized. But what really disturbed the experts was that the teeth were *dredged up,* which indicated they were on the surface of the sea floor and may have been recently deposited there! Older teeth, they said, would have been covered by so much silt that the dredging gear in those days would not have snagged them.

Could I find such teeth in our area, or would they be buried beneath tons of overburden? I figured that if the small teeth were being washed up out of the bottom by the currents and the surf, perhaps so too were the large ones.

As I continued swimming out from shore, going deeper, staying just above the bottom, I suddenly saw ahead of me a jumbled pile of rocks. I glanced at my depth gauge: I was twenty-five feet underwater.

I eased up to the scattering of small boulders and looked them over. At first glance there appeared to be parts of old branches and six-inch-thick logs scattered around the area, some sticking up vertically out of the surrounding clay bottom.

On closer examination, however, I realized this was not wood I was looking at, because the pieces were hard as stone. I rolled over a chunk that looked as if it would have fitted nicely in a fireplace. Was it a petrified log? I tapped it with the blade of my knife; it sent forth a hard, almost metallic ring.

I picked up another piece with more projections and a slightly larger than thumb-size hole through one end. Brushing off a layer of silt, I held the object close to my mask and studied its brown surface. Part of it was smooth and slightly grooved, but the end appeared to have been recently broken. As I puzzled over the peculiar pattern of tiny cellular pockets that showed at the break, it suddenly dawned on me that I was looking at a fossilized bone! Where it was broken I was seeing the cellular structure of bone marrow—something I had noticed years before when looking over a collection of prehistoric bones in a museum at Bartow, Florida.

I went back to the section that looked like a long piece of firewood and reexamined it. When I saw that it had no cellular pores my heart started beating in double time. "My God," I thought, "this has to be fossil ivory! A section of mammoth or mastodon tusk!" Chunks of it lay all over the place, as did the bones. Looking around with new awareness at objects I had earlier thought to be nothing but waterlogged branches or odd-shaped rocks, I now recognized them for what they were. I was sitting smack in the middle of a prehistoric boneyard!

Eagerly I started grabbing chunks and piling them up, building a cairn of the pieces I wanted to salvage. It was incredible. I was like a kid in a candy store. It seemed as if everything I looked at now was either bone or tusk. Was the latter really ivory? I didn't know. Had to have been once, but I had no idea what fossilizing did to it.

I overturned rocks and fanned at things with both hands until clouds of sediment billowed about me as thick as smoke. Finally I had to move off a few feet to find clear water to see well enough to start all over again. One minute I was trying to free a giant curved rib bone, the next I was struggling to dig out part of a huge femur more than half as long as I was. And everywhere I uncovered slightly different diameters of tusk—so many fragments the whole thing must have been fifteen feet long

. . . or were there two or more tusks? If I had found a pile of gold coins I couldn't have been more excited. It was like stumbling onto the legendary elephant graveyard, and I was probably the first human to lay eyes on it in more than a million years.

In my eager fanning and upending of rocks I almost overlooked an object with the shape, feel and color of a nondescript rock the size of a small loaf of bread. But in turning it over I recognized the parallel pattern of curves along its flat surface as if thick flat-ended bone plates were fused together in one long lump. It was a mammoth's molar.

I couldn't believe my luck in finding all of these things. Quickly I started loading the large nylon-mesh goody bag I had clipped to my weight belt. The bag couldn't begin to hold even a fraction of the pieces I had stacked up, so I selected the ones that looked most interesting and left the rest, scattering them among the rocks again so they would not be too obvious in case another diver chanced upon the site. I knew I'd have no trouble finding the place again, but I was surprised it had not already been found and picked over.

As I was about ready to drag my heavy bag of bones back to shore I took one last look around. For some reason, perhaps because they seemed out of place and were much lighter colored than the surrounding dark brown rocks and clay, two large barnacles caught my eye. They were stuck on something, and out of curiosity I ran the blade of my knife under one edge and flipped the object over.

What came out of the silt in a puff of mud was not a piece of old metal boat bottom as I had suspected or a slab of pier piling. There lay what I had been searching for—a perfectly shaped jet black triangular shark's tooth at least five inches long!

I snatched it up as if I'd found a gold ingot, turning it over and over in my hands, feeling the smooth, heavy hardness of it, the still comparatively keen serrated edges undulled all these millions of years—a tooth from *Carcharodon megalodon,* the 100-foot prehistoric monster.

The barnacles were solidly attached to the tooth's enamel. There was nothing prehistoric about them. But they meant that this tooth had been exposed rather than buried, at least long enough for the barnacles to decide that it would make a satisfactory foundation for their shell homes—if such creatures gave thought to this selection.

I searched the general area to see if I could find any more big shark teeth but there were none.

With the kind of luck I was having I wouldn't have been surprised to have uncovered the skeleton of a caveman "done in" by the mammoth before his demise.

Realizing finally that I had just enough air left to get me and my burden of bones and teeth back to the beach, I reluctantly decided it was time to go. Could I *surely* find the place again?

Leaving the bag on the bottom, I finned up to the surface and took a visual bearing on a couple of motels and other prominent landmarks back on the beach so there would be no doubt that I could relocate the place. Then I dove back down to my bag of goodies and started the long, laborious swim ashore.

Those first finds exceeded my greatest expectations. At home where I could examine them more closely, it appeared that I had indeed stumbled into a prehistoric graveyard. More animals than just the big mammoth had apparently come to an end here. Some of the fragments I had collected but been unable to identify underwater turned out to be the fossil teeth of a beaver, a vertebra from the backbone of a whale, and various large shell sections belonging to a prehistoric land tortoise. I could hardly wait to get back there again.

In the months that followed I dove the area many times when the conditions were good, and often when water conditions were bad. Customarily I would spend six hours a day diving off Venice Beach. In all that time I found an incredible number of fossils, the remains of virtually every prehistoric animal that ever roamed Florida thousands of years ago.

For a long time I found bones that had belonged to huge animals. Since I had read that Florida had no dinosaurs in its prehistoric past, these animals had to be mammoths and giant ground sloths, the latter an animal that perhaps stood twelve feet tall when it reared up on its massive hind limbs to feed on lofty vegetation. From my research I knew that authorities thought both of these animals had lived in Florida about 10,000 years ago, when they were then believed to have become extinct.

One day while I was working a sand bottom near an ancient limestone reef along the front of Venice Beach I dug up an object about the size of my fist. At first I thought it was a piece of coal. Then I saw what it really was and almost swallowed my mouthpiece in surprise. There was no need to brush off this item; it was already clean. Even in the half-light of that depth I could see gray-black cusps, smooth and gleaming. It was a mastodon tooth with some of its root shafts still intact.

What a variety of prehistoric animals must have perished in this relatively small area. Along with the remains of mammoths, I now had the mastodon. Both animals were early ancestors of our present-day elephant, and both lived during the Pleistocene period, one million years ago.

In the same sedimentary beds as the prehistoric animal bones I found literally hundreds of huge fossil shark teeth from three to six inches long; I didn't count those under three inches. Indeed, my diving log shows that over a period of years of intermittent diving in the offshore waters along Venice Beach, I recovered at least 2,000 of the giant *Carcharodon megalodon* shark teeth completely intact, plus several thousand broken fragments of others, some of which showed evidence of having been worked or shaped as tools by early man. What puzzled me was finding the shark teeth in the same deposits as the mammoth remains. Was the giant shark, believed by many scientists to have become extinct twelve million years ago, still swimming in these seas as recently as 10,000 or 11,000 years ago when mammoths roamed the Florida shores? Or was *megalodon* around even more recent than that?

Seeing the relationship of all these bones with the shark teeth, my impression was that the mammoths had died before the sea level came up and deposited the clay beds over their bones. The presence of the shark teeth in these clay beds indicated to me that the 80- to 100-foot *Carcharodon megalodon* was still living *after* the mammoths, 8,000 to 10,000 years ago, which could conceivably mean that these giant sharks were still around at the same time as early man!

I soon realized that the area in twenty feet of water off Venice Beach was actually part of an ancient swamp bottom, with the tree stumps still firmly rooted in old muck and peat deposits. Did this explain what these great land animals were doing there? During the time of the rising and falling of sea levels between the ice ages, had many of the animals become mired in this muck as they had in the La Brea Tar Pits near Los Angeles, California?

I suspected that they had, and that the level of the sea had eventually risen and covered them, completely hiding them from man's sight until, by accident, I found the site many centuries later.

Of all the bones and teeth I recovered from the boneyard, I gave most away to various museums or to friends. Many of the choicer finds I turned over to the University of Michigan, which helped identify bones unfamiliar to me.

Carbon dating some of the wood from this ancient bottom could establish a date.*

At the time I wanted to introduce others to the sport of diving so I formed a diving club in Venice called the Dolphin Divers and proceeded to teach whoever was interested. There were no organizations to certify divers then, so we learned as we dove, making mistakes and learning from them.

Before long every diver in the area knew about the offshore bonanza and worked it for bone collections of

---

*In 1962 scientists got radiocarbon dates from similar stumps rooted in the ocean bottom forty-five feet below sea level near Panama City, Florida, and found they were over 36,000 years old.

their own. Local gift shops still do a booming business in such unique items as whole or fragmentary fossil shark teeth. And even today, after all these years, the Gulf bottom offshore from Venice Beach still provides an occasional giant *megalodon* tooth for divers patient enough to search this remarkable four-fathom prehistoric boneyard.

PART TWO

The Springs

11

~~~~~~~~~~~~~ *bones of contention*

DURING THE winter months the Gulf of Mexico became too cold to dive and we had to find another area. I'd heard that a few miles east of Venice was an unusual warm mineral spring, a health spa where people from all over the world were attracted by 87° highly mineralized waters.

I drove down and talked to the springs' manager, Sam Herron, explaining to him that we had a diving club in Venice and asking permission to bring some of our club members down for training in his "heated pool."

Mr. Herron said, "Sure, I'll be glad to have your club use our springs." So that solved our problem.

Warm Mineral Springs is in a beautifully landscaped setting. Once you pass through the gift shop, snack bar and bathhouses you see palm trees, tropical plants and a wide, gently sloping lawn surrounding a quiet pool several hundred feet in diameter. From the surface it looks like a neatly tailored, shallow, man-made lake. But the only thing man-made about the springs is an encircling sand wading beach extending underwater several yards out from shore to a depth of five feet for the convenience of bathers. Beyond a buoy line, Mother Nature takes over and the depth drops off sharply to over 200 feet.

Our first dive was a great sensation. The water was warm despite a fairly low air temperature that morning. After free diving awhile, a couple of us slipped on our tanks, waded out to the buoy line and went down with scuba.

The water was clear, with a greenish-yellow cast. The bottom dropped away so quickly it was like stepping off a balcony into liquid space. The overhead sunlight did not penetrate well as we slowly sank in the 200-foot abyss beneath us. I watched the cavern walls as we descended. They were covered with a thick purple-black, tough-skinned slime caused, I later learned, by the minerals in the water. It was unlike anything I had seen before.

Suddenly about twenty-five feet down the wall appeared to turn into peculiar long pendants. I stopped my descent and approached closer. Was this some odd slime formation?

I reached out and touched one of the shapes. It was

smooth stone. Behind it were others—some three and four feet long, some so thick I could not have reached around them with my arms. The shapes hung from the ceiling in a kind of undercut wall recess that stretched off in both directions. Beside me my diving buddy was equally perplexed. When I looked at him he simply shrugged. I moved up between the rock forms and looked closely at their surfaces. They were smooth with a flowing form, and as my hand glided over the surface of one of them it came to me what they were—stalactites, dripstones that form in dry caves.

Dry caves! Then what the devil were they doing here twenty-five feet underwater? Was it possible that the water level in the spring was once so low that these formed?

Not only possible, I decided, but that had to have been the cause. There was no other way for it to happen.

My diving buddy snapped me out of my contemplation of the peculiar formations with a tap on the shoulder and a finger pointed downward. He was eager to get on with the dive.

We eased down through the darkening water, seeing more smooth vertical walls of purple slime. In some places great slabs of it had sloughed off, leaving ragged edges around the wound.

By the time we reached a ledge at forty-five feet we had snapped on our waterproof flashlights. They were only good for a limited time before they shorted out, but in their dim yellow beams we saw that the ledges were covered with loose black sediment four inches to four feet deep. We continued down to sixty feet and there, back in a small cave, we saw more stalactites! Moving back from the wall I turned my light downward. The slender yellow shaft revealed nothing but the black maw of the watery pit below. What was down there, I wondered?

That evening, November 26, 1958, I wrote letters to the geology departments of several universities throughout the state telling them that we had discovered stalactites in the spring from twenty-five to sixty-five feet underwater, which indicated that this area was dry at one time. I wrote: "To the best of my knowledge, this would be the first positive proof that this part of Florida, probably during the last Ice Age, was this far above sea level, and a dry cave for thousands of years, but due to my not being a professional geologist, I would appreciate your advising me if these findings have been proven prior to this date, and if not, would your department be interested in further investigation and research on this subject?"

Eventually I received responses. Two schools said they did not have time to send geologists to examine the formations. However, Harold Kelly Brooks, a geologist from the University of Florida at Gainesville, wrote to say that he was keenly interested in exploring the springs. "Your discovery is unusual and I am most grateful to you for bringing it to my attention," said Brooks. "Though it is generally known that sea level was lowered by about 300 feet during the great advances of Pleistocene ice, the geological features produced at this time have not been recorded sufficiently in the scientific literature. . . ." He congratulated me on making this unique discovery and said he would be down as soon as he could to see them. Brooks mentioned that he had been diving for five years and during that time had searched a number of other springs and underwater caverns for stalactites and stalagmites without success. From the tone of his letter he sounded genuinely excited about our find.

Meanwhile I kept hearing about another lost spring somewhere nearby, one that was far back in the prairie-and-jungle property belonging to the Mackle Brothers Land Developing Company. It was called Little Salt Spring, but nobody seemed to know exactly where it was. The back country was big and sprawling, with parts unexplored. It was a large sea of wild grasses and weeds interspersed with dense islands of cabbage palms, vines and palmettos. Only a few meandering trails (they could hardly be called roads) went in there, and penetration was difficult because the prairies were often flooded. But from the little information I had gathered, I thought perhaps we could find the spring.

With that in mind, some friends and I set off in a jeep one weekend to search for it. Accompanying me were divers Bob Chapman, Norman Rack and Luanna Pettay, a young anthropologist who had recently received her Ph.D. Although Luanna dived, she was not able to do much of it because of sinus problems.

Our exploratory trip took us into country where it was hard to believe we were only a few miles from civilization. Part of the land was as high and dry as a western prairie. But a foot or two drop in elevation put us into the water table: The prairie turned marshy, with birds, beasts and reptiles scattering every which way while we splashed and skidded through. As hammock after hammock of dense vegetation passed and we alternated from dry prairie to flooded flatlands crisscrossed with game trails, I got a strong impression of what it must have been like in the early days to motor across the more difficult parts of Africa's Serengeti Plain. If an impala had suddenly bounded out of the grass beside us, I doubt if we'd have flinched.

For two days we searched without success, returning to civilization each night wet, mud-spattered and thoroughly bushed. Then, on the third day, acting on a tip from a friend and remarkably fine sixty-four-year-old diver, Iris Woolcock, we found it. Iris put us on a trail that came within 1,000 feet of the spring. And it was a good thing she knew it was there or we'd easily have bypassed it.

It was in open prairie country but hidden in the heart of a jungle hammock so thick it was difficult to worm our way in carrying our diving gear. When we broke through the vegetation and saw that quiet round pool of dark water several hundred feet across, we were sweaty and tired but elated.

Little Salt Spring was certainly in a different setting than the lushly landscaped Warm Mineral Springs. Here we stood in mud up to our knees, swatting mosquitoes and yellow flies in a solid wall of jungle while watching high-flying buzzards reflected in the pool's ominous black waters. Somewhere under that mirrored surface there lurked, we were told, at least two decidedly unfriendly alligators.

But we had come to dive. Although it was too late to accomplish much, Norman, Bob and I slipped on our gear and plowed waist deep through muck that reeked of the sulfur smell of rotten eggs, to tumble into tepid water that tasted as bad as it smelled.

Beneath the surface the water was clear with a slightly

brown color to it. We found that the upper part of the pool was shaped like a large bowl with a hole precisely in the middle of its bottom. We explored the bottom down to forty-five feet, where it dropped off vertically to a depth we later learned was about 220 feet. In the dim beams of our flashlights we saw that everything was covered with loose sediment, so loose that the slightest movement of a swim fin six feet above caused a tornado of fine silt to swirl into the water like smoke.

Since there were no ledges above forty-five feet in the spring, there were no stalactites above this depth. But we dove through the hole in the bottom of the basin, and just under that overhang we found the same kind of dripstone formations that were in Warm Mineral Springs. Because the massive shapes could only form in a dry cave, the water level of Little Salt Spring had to have been at least forty-five feet below its present level. And if my suspicions were correct, the stalactites dated back to the last Ice Age when so much of the earth's water was frozen in glaciers and, as geologist Brooks had said, sea level was generally thought to be 300 feet lower.

Had early man lived in these dry caverns? It seemed logical to me. They had inhabited the caverns of Europe; why not these?

On my last trip up from the overhang I paused to fan the sediments on the forty-five-foot ledge. As the loose material billowed around me, I glimpsed a small bone lying on the rock ledge. Picking it up I headed for the surface.

Stumbling ashore, wallowing once more through the evil-smelling muck, I turned the bone over and over in my hand, examining it.

Luanna could hardly wait for us to tell what we had

seen. I held out my find to her. "What do you say, Luanna . . . animal or human?"

She took it and looked at it carefully. "Oh yes," she said. "This is human . . . part of a femur, I think. But it must be recent. Maybe someone fell in and drowned."

On the way home that evening, bouncing and jolting our way out of the back country, I asked Luanna if there was any possibility that the bone could be much older than we thought. I said, "If the spring was a dry cavern 10,000 to 20,000 years ago, then why couldn't this bone have belonged to some early inhabitant?"

"Oh, I don't really think so," said Luanna. "You see, Bill, if the cavern was dry that many years ago there wouldn't have been any humans here then. Humans have only been in Florida for perhaps 4,000 years. I'm sure this bone isn't over 100 years old at most."

Maybe Luanna was right. After all, she was an anthropologist. Still, I wasn't persuaded.

A few days later we returned to Little Salt. Despite Luanna's sinus problems, she finally agreed to dive with me. We descended to the ledge at forty-five feet and after fanning our way through the sediments we found dozens of human bones—tibias, femurs, humeri—scattered all over the place. Most were in pretty good condition. Luanna was impressed but still clung to her original belief that the bones were not too old.

Harold Kelly Brooks, the young assistant professor of geology at the University of Florida, finally came down to dive in both springs to see the stalactites. A couple of months earlier I had left half a dozen pieces of broken stalactites at his office so he could examine them before he came down.

When we came up from our dive at Warm Mineral several newspaper reporters were there to ask him what he thought about the formations. Brooks showed them pieces he had broken off from the overhang, but all he was willing to say to the press was that he could not make up his mind what the formations were until he had a better opportunity to examine them.

Considering what he had just seen in the springs, I thought this was a strange attitude for him to take. Hadn't he already had a chance to examine the pieces of stalactites I had left in his office?

Later that evening at our home Brooks was talking with Peggy Bogert, whom he did not realize was a reporter for the Venice *Gondolier*. He said, "I'm not sure that they're stalactites. I haven't had an opportunity to look them over closely."

I asked Brooks how one could be certain. He said, "Every stalactite has a small hole through the center of it." He then went on to explain that stalactites started forming as a tiny strawlike shape of calcium carbonate. Water percolating through the earth above picks up small dissolved quantities of lime present in the soil. As this water flows through the straw it becomes supersaturated on exposure to air and deposits more calcium carbonate, or calcite, until the straw formation thickens. Over a long period of time the formation grows into an elongated column of sometimes considerable proportions. A stalagmite, the cone-shaped column formed on the floor of a cave from the constant dripping of the supersaturated lime water from an overhead stalactite, has no hole in its center.

I said, "Well, if that's the case, let's look at some of the broken stalactites from the springs that I have in the garage." We all trooped out there. I broke one in two and there it was—the bore hole in its center.

Even faced with this, Brooks was unwilling to admit publicly that the formations were stalactites. While his actions were a complete mystery to me then, I learned the reason sometime later when he wrote to me: ". . . It seems everyone wants to get into the act. I am publicity shy for the simple reason that one cannot trust reports [reporters?] and science does not lend itself to sensationalism. . . ."

Many years later, after Brooks had earned his Ph.D. in geology, he did acknowledge in a letter to me and in scientific papers ". . . that the deposits in the spring are definitely dripstone and there is a secondary deposit of spring travertine. The dripstone indicates a lower sea level and probably dates from 11,000 to slightly greater than 20,000 years. . . ."

Despite the exciting things we had found in Little Salt Spring, the difficulty of carrying all our heavy diving gear in there dampened our enthusiasm to dive it, at least for the time being. On the other hand, Warm Mineral Springs was convenient, comfortable and still unexplored. When Genie Clark heard about the stalactites there she was anxious to see them for herself. She had dived the springs before I had come back to Florida, but apparently she had not gone deep enough to see the formations below twenty-five feet. She had been interested in studying some small fish that swam near the surface. Oddly enough, none of these fish strayed far down into the springs for, as we later learned, they were confined to the surface where there was dissolved oxygen. Below fifteen feet the highly mineralized water of the springs lacked oxygen and therefore would not have sustained the fish.

Genie joined me at Warm Mineral Springs and was most impressed when she saw the stalactites. She agreed that it was entirely possible that when this was a dry cave early man might have sought shelter there.

I decided to do some personal investigating in Warm Mineral. As I descended alone to have a look around, I soon realized that the visibility was going to be terrible. The heavy purplish black slime and thick brown sediments absorbed all natural light. But on this particular dive under the overhang I noticed two large lumps on the shelf that piqued my curiosity. I wondered if they were stalactites that had fallen from the overhang sometime in the distant past. Moving close to them, I fanned away the sediments. The yellow gleam of my flashlight revealed the dark brown surface of stalactites about four or five feet long, exactly like the formations that grew down from the roof above.

I continued excavating down between the two heavy formations to an opening just barely wide enough to admit my hands. Squeezing my hands through the narrow crevice, I touched what felt like hard-packed leaves. Pushing further, my fingers probing into this leafy material, I touched two bones that I recovered and brought to the surface to show Luanna.

I felt sure these were human tibias, shinbones. But Luanna was not sure. She wanted to be certain, so we took the bones to her parents' house where she left them outdoors on a stump to dry. The next morning when she went back for them she found that one had been carried off by a neighbor's dog!

I claimed the one remaining bone even though

Luanna was still not positive it was human.

The temptation to explore Little Salt Spring grew too strong. Despite all the hardships of getting our equipment in to that bleak hole, we returned for another look.

Again we found large numbers of apparently human bones, recovering twenty or thirty specimens in the hope that they would shed more light on their age and origin. Luanna was really excited over our finds but still reserved judgment because she wasn't sure.

"Bill, the bones are in excellent condition, but I'm not positive they're human. If they are, I simply don't believe they're as old as you think. I can't tell you anything more than that. I'm not qualified to assess them. To my knowledge nothing like this has ever been found before."

"But listen, Luanna," I argued, "the bones in Warm Mineral Springs must be Ice Age material. They were back in the cavern beneath broken stalactites under the overhang. There's no possible way they could have gotten back there underwater unless they did so when the cave was dry."

"No, no, there must be another explanation," she insisted. "They had to have gotten there much later. Alligators may have dragged them under the overhang. I don't know. Why don't you contact Dr. John Goggin? He's the professor of anthropology at the University of Florida in Gainesville. He's the only diving archaeologist in the country. He should examine the bones *in situ* and evaluate them."

"All right," I said, "that's a good idea. Let's get hold of Dr. Goggin."

Luanna telephoned him that night, telling him about our discoveries. Dr. Goggin sounded enthusiastic, so much so that he said he would come down the next day with a group of his students who were diving archaeologists "in training."

Great! At last a qualified authority would have an opportunity to evaluate these things and maybe we could get at the truth. I realized that Luanna was reluctant to make any judgment because although she was an anthropologist, she as yet didn't have sufficient stature among the well-known professionals in the field to attract any recognition of the finds. And too, at the moment, everything was speculative, based entirely on my feeling that these were very old bones. I suppose I wouldn't have felt so sure of this had it not been for the stalactites and the location of the bones back under the overhang in an area where they were not likely to have gotten in this flooded cavern.

Luanna had accepted a job teaching anthropology at Ohio State University, but before she left she made arrangements for Dr. Goggin and his crew of diving students to come down that Friday night. Between the two of us we found places for everyone to sleep. I rounded up a jeep to lead our small caravan into Little Salt Spring. Because of the large number of human bones there, I thought we should tackle it first. But as luck would have it, before the group arrived it started to rain.

It rained so long and so hard that by the next morning the cattle trail we had to follow to the spring was flooded. We sloshed our way through in my jeep and four other loaded vehicles, and in addition to all our diving gear had brought a small boat to serve as a diving platform. It was raining so hard we could almost have used the boat to get us across the flooded countryside on the way to the spring.

I had located an old dock on the north side of the pool

basin, but it was in such terrible condition that before you got in the water to dive you sank almost waist deep in the aromatic muck. Consequently it was a long time before we got everyone geared up and into the water.

By then it was late afternoon and it started to rain again.

It was my impression that this was supposed to be a scientifically controlled dive, but to my amazement Dr. Goggin let his students run rampant in the spring. After being on the forty-five-foot ledge for a while they came to the surface with their pockets, shirts, hands and arms full of bones, human bones—leg bones, arm bones, jaw bones, pieces of skulls—so many bones that they looked like grave robbers on a spree. All the finds were dumped into our small boat until the bottom of it was deep in human bones.

Dr. Goggin was impressed. But he thought the material was only 500 or 600 years old.

That night, over several martinis, we discussed the finds further. I showed the anthropologist one of the two bones I'd found in Warm Mineral Springs (we never recovered the one the dog stole).

Goggin said, "Of course it's part of a human tibia. Where did you find it?"

I told him that it was one of two I had recovered from leaf sediments beneath a couple of fallen stalactites under the overhang.

"Hmmm, that's interesting," he said. "But really, I don't feel that it can be more than 500 years old, Bill. I wish I had more time to really study these two springs, but most of my time has been tied up either at the university or with investigations of old Spanish shipwrecks."

Luanna and I were both discouraged. We had counted on Dr. Goggin to really get things moving and to bring about a complete and thorough scientific investigation of our finds.

"I simply can't believe that the bones are that young," I told him. "I feel sure they're Ice Age material."

"What are you talking about?" Dr. Goggin said sharply. "Are you an archaeologist?" he asked me. "Are you a geologist?"

"No, I don't pretend to be. That's why I asked you to come down here and dive to see for yourself. It just seems so logical to me . . . I can see no other explanation. The bones were back under the overhang, in leaf beds under fallen stalactites. How could they possibly have gotten back there except in a dry cave? And if the cave was only dry during the forming of those stalactites 10,-000 to 20,000 years ago, then doesn't it follow that they couldn't possibly be of recent origin?"

Dr. Goggin stared at me. He was upset to think that I presumed to know anything about these scientific matters, and he didn't mind telling me so.

Just before going to bed that night I asked him again about the possibility of taking over the exploration of Little Salt and Warm Mineral Springs. He assured me he didn't have time to do it. I knew he didn't believe anything I'd told him. But what he didn't know was that he was turning his back on one of the most important archaeological finds in the Western Hemisphere. That night we did not part the best of friends.

Next morning it was still raining. The whole group drove down to Warm Mineral Springs hoping that when we got there the rain would stop. It didn't. Even from the surface the water looked bad. I made a quick dive down to be sure, but it didn't take long for me to see that the five inches of rain we'd had in the last twenty-four hours had washed so much soil into the springs that it was impossible to see anything. Nor would the lights that divers had then have helped. The beams were simply reflected back from the particles in the water.

Dr. Goggin decided not to take his students into the water and told us he would be back some other time.

I never saw him again.

12

~~~~~~~~~~ *down the sink and into the drain*

WHEN I REALIZED that our efforts to interest qualified scientists in the two sites had failed, I decided to go on and explore both springs myself. The State of Florida had not been interested, nor were the universities to whom I had written letters describing our finds. Consequently, as we found more interesting material in the springs we received a lot of newspaper publicity. As a result, Dr. Goggin repudiated everything that we said about our discoveries and told the press we were nothing but amateurs who had no business making any claims.

As our finds received more publicity, large numbers of scuba divers were constantly contacting me and asking me to take them into the springs. As often as possible I took them down. However, I was working as a contractor then, building houses on speculation, and had to spend most of my time at that job. But whenever I had a few hours to spare I would dive in one or the other of the springs.

On one trip I took Dr. Eugenie Clark and Bill Stephens along with us to dive Little Salt Spring. We dove down to the forty-five-foot ledge and recovered a number of bones that Genie brought up for Luanna Pettay to examine. Bill had one of the best underwater cameras made at that time, and he was able to get an excellent photographic record of our dives.

Since Luanna was an anthropologist, Genie urged her to write a scientific article on our finds up to that point. Genie, Luanna and I discussed what we had found so far at the forty-five-foot level, and we decided to make a deep dive in Little Salt to find out just what was in the bottom.

We set up the dive and invited other experienced divers to participate in the project with us. The group included Dr. Saunders, a Gainesville veterinarian who had been diving with his friend Ken Howe for several years and had made interesting finds of prehistoric animal bones and Indian artifacts in other springs; Tom McQuarrie, owner of the Crystal River AquaPier Dive Shop; Dr. Jarl Malwin, a Venice dentist and amateur archaeologist; Luanna Pettay; Howard Barefoot; Ken

Henne; Charlie Carneal and his wife; Norman Rack; Bud Kraft; Genie Clark; Bill and Peggy Stephens; and my wife at that time, Muriel Royal. Quite a sizable expedition.

We discussed the dive beforehand and I knew that only a few of the most experienced divers would be making the deep dive. The rest would maintain our base of operations or act as safety divers. Apparently I was the only one in the group who had dived to over 200 feet, but since the others were experienced I expected no trouble.

We decided that Genie Clark and Bill Stephens would make the descent with me and attempt to reach bottom. Bud Kraft and Charlie Carneal would act as safety divers. Dr. Saunders and Howard Barefoot would be standing by on the surface. We had anchored a boat in the center of the spring and dropped an anchor line down to about 220 feet. Kraft would station himself on the line about 100 feet down and remain there in case we needed assistance.

Stephens was using a double-hose regulator, as we all were in those days. However, he had had some trouble with the equipment when one of his accordian rubber hoses developed a crack. Stephens patched it the night before with tape, hoping it would hold.

Genie and I wore double-tanks and Stephens wore a single tank but carried a spare and a regulator under his arm. We each carried lights. We agreed that no matter what happened we would not let go of the anchor line.

We started down the line, with me going first, Genie following, Stephens and Kraft bringing up the rear. About fifty feet down we lost all overhead light and switched on our flashlights. After that it was a long, liquid descent through the blackness pierced only by the probing yellow beams of our lights.

At 100 feet Kraft stopped his descent to wait for us there. A few feet below him my trusty light suddenly went out. I banged it but there was no hope. I signaled to the others what my problem was and went back to the surface for another light.

As I descended again I met the others coming up. Once more we all started back down the descent line with me leading.

After a while we stopped and everyone checked my depth gauges. I had one strapped on each wrist so that we could doublecheck our depth. Both read 130 feet. We continued down.

This was to be just a brief exploratory dive to the bottom, a quick look around and then back to the surface. I planned to go down into the bottom sediments to see if I could feel any bones.

When we reached bottom the only way I could tell we were there was in the gradual thickening of the water from suspended particles of sediment. The depth gauges read 220 feet. I glanced up and saw the lights of both divers just above me, so I continued down into the sediments, feeling around blindly since my light was useless in that black soup.

Finally I felt the soup thicken to muck. Carefully I felt through it as far as I could reach while still clinging with one hand to the rope. But I touched no bones, just velvet soft muck. Finally I decided to get out of the stuff and go up where I had left Genie and Stephens.

Following the line back up out of the sediments, I saw no lights above me. I shined mine up the line. Both of my companions had disappeared. They were gone!

That shook me. Genie was hardly more than a month out of the hospital after having her fourth baby. I thought something serious had happened because all of us had agreed not to let go of the rope. We were over 200 feet down in a sinkhole that was blacker than the bottom of an inkwell. The chances of getting back to the surface on our own without getting lost or caught under the overhang were slim.

I shined my light around and saw nothing but its reflected yellow glow in the silt particles. Thinking that maybe my friends were still on the line above me, I started up. About then my light went out.

While I've never had nitrogen narcosis despite the fact that I have dived to about 250 feet, I became concerned that maybe my companions had had narcosis problems. When I was unable to see them after going quite a way up the line, I was more sure than ever that Genie and Stephens had let go of the line and were lost somewhere in the bottom of the spring.

Then I saw our safety man, Bud Kraft, at the 100-foot depth. He motioned me to go up.

When I broke water I was relieved to see that Genie and Bill Stephens were in the boat. They both acted just as glad to see me. As I climbed aboard with them, I noticed that Bill was bleeding from the nose, but it was apparently nothing serious. Genie said that shortly after we checked our depth gauge at 130 feet she had begun to feel the effects of nitrogen narcosis. She remembered looking at someone's depth gauge but couldn't see it well enough to tell what time it was. In fact, she hadn't really cared what time it was.

A bit further down the line she felt as if someone had opened a window and let fresh air into her stuffy room. The air she breathed seemed so fresh it made her light-headed. At this point, Genie remembered, the water visibility suddenly changed. She began to see millions of floating black particles around her. Shining her light down, all she could see of me, she said, was one of my hands sticking up out of the silt, still clenching the rope.

Under the effects of nitrogen narcosis she had the impression that I was already dead. Apparently it was not a disturbing thought. As she said, she just felt "sweet sadness." She reached down to touch my hand but found she could not reach me.

When she began to enjoy the rhythmic sound of her regulator, under the impression that she was in the hospital delivery room and the anesthetist was telling her to take a deep breath, Genie realized something was wrong with her thinking.

Dimly aware now that she was being affected by nitrogen narcosis, and remembering that she had once heard that a diver under narcosis might remove his regulator in the belief that he could breathe without it, she reached up and held her regulator tightly in her mouth. At least she still had the presence of mind to keep a firm grip on the rope.

She looked above her for Bill Stephens and saw that he was gone. She shined her light around in the water but was unable to see him. Thinking that Bill was perhaps above her on the rope, she swam upward, sliding her hand along the line, searching for him.

When Genie realized that he was not in her immediate vicinity she stopped, perplexed, feeling very alone in the darkness where both of her companions, it seemed, had abandoned her.

At that point she lost her sense of up and down and couldn't decide which way she was to go on the rope. It was the only tangible thing she had to hold on to in that inky void, but still she could not tell which way was up.

Finally she remembered that I had told her if she was ever in this predicament and was unable to see her bubbles ascending, she should take off her weight belt and hold it out in front of her. If the weight belt stood up straight from her hand, she was to turn around and go in the other direction. But rather than unbuckle her belt, Genie felt her bubbles with her hand and decided which way was up and which was down. She started in the direction she thought was up. A minute later she realized she was enjoying those long dreamy blasts of fresh air again. Instead of going up she had gone down and was feeling the narcosis again.

This time Genie turned around on the rope. Although still feeling sort of sad that I was down there in all that muck below her, she simply had to get out of the depths that were causing her to think so peculiarly. This time when she headed up she followed the line to the surface.

Bill Stephens' experiences were not too different. Apparently just before reaching bottom Stephens, who was the third person on the line, ran out of air. It became apparent to him that he was feeling the effects of narcosis when he found it almost impossible to remove one regulator from his mouth and insert the regulator from his spare tank. In doing so, the spare tank slipped out of his hands.

Suddenly Stephens was enveloped in bubbles gushing

up around him. Thinking that he was hallucinating from the narcosis, he started up the line. Actually, when the tank slid out of his hands, the stress on his accordian air hose tore the tape off his "repair" job and the air poured out of the cracked hose, rushing up around him toward the surface.

Following the bubbles, Stephens made a hurried ascent, fortunate to have escaped the situation with nothing more than a minor nosebleed.

When we finally got together on the surface and compared our experiences, everyone was relieved that it was not more serious.

Shortly after this the Mackle Brothers closed Little Salt Spring to divers unless they signed a waiver that released the Mackle Corporation from any responsibilities in the event of diver injury or fatality. Finally the Mackle Brothers had so much trouble with cars getting stuck in the flooded pastures leading to the spring that they closed the area to diving entirely.

I had permission to walk in if I wanted to dive, which I did on at least four occasions. I can't say it was the most enjoyable walk I've ever made since it was two miles to the spring in water often knee-deep, and I had to carry my tank and other gear on my back. You can see why I didn't do that too often.

Usually I went in with mask, fins and knife to free-dive. But one of the times when I had full scuba gear with me I was interested in an area where a friend of mine had found a very fine point. I returned to this site and excavated, hand-fanning down through the sediments, and found a skull in perfect condition. Within thirty inches of it I found a beautiful spear point, a stone knife, six arrowheads, several scrapers and a piece of worked shell dipper. All of these artifacts I later gave to Dr. Reynold Ruppé of Arizona State University at Tempe, so the items could be studied and better evaluated. These artifacts have since been turned over to Carl Clausen, Director of the General Development Foundation, who is in charge of the Little Salt exploration. Oddly enough, these were the only points that have been recovered from the spring.

On this particular trip I dived below a seventy-foot ledge, looked up and could see the surface. This was quite remarkable because most days the sun shining on the highly mineralized water creates a milky condition and consequently poor visibility. I swam under a ledge and about forty feet back into a cave beneath it that had a ceiling flat as a pancake. Strangely, to this day no one has ever found that ledge again. But I feel this cave goes back at least 100 feet.

I made about three more trips to Little Salt carrying just my basic free-diving gear. Invariably I was alone because none of my friends were willing to make that long hike just to go diving. On one such trip I dove down to the bottom at thirty feet, and there, to my surprise, lay a sleeping alligator, right on the spot where I wanted to work.

I knew there was one way to get him to move and maybe get a ride out of it too. Carefully I came up from behind him and reached around his neck.

He came to with a jerk and took off in a cloud of silt, with me hanging on for dear life. I got my legs around his body and away we went toward the surface. It wasn't as thrilling as riding a shark, but at least I got him to move off the spot I had selected. I also got my arms sliced up a bit from the sharp scutes around the gator's neck.

Finally Dr. Goggin prevailed upon the Mackle Brothers to close the spring altogether to divers. A perimeter fence was erected around the pasture and its gate was to be kept locked. But in time divers cut down a section of the fence in a remote area and often drove in with a jeep.

I have no idea how many bones have been taken from the spring, but from those I have seen I would conservatively estimate that in the upper pool down to the forty-five-foot ledge we were dealing with the remains of several hundred human beings. No one knows why they were there, but apparently Dr. Goggin planned to return in the future to find out. Before he did, however, the career of this already distinguished forty-six-year-old archaeologist came to a tragic and untimely end in 1963 when he died of cancer.

13

~~~~~~~ sabertooth cavern and ponce de león

MENTION A SPRING and most people will think of a steady flow of water from a small hole in the ground that creates a modest pool a few feet wide from which they may drink some of the coolest, clearest water that has ever touched their lips.

When most Floridians think of a spring, they usually think of something quite different. They think of a clear crystalline pool from several hundred feet to several hundred yards in diameter, often with a middle "boil" or raised welt of water caused by an upwelling of thousands of gallons of cool spring water. If they were to look below the spring's mirrored surface, they would see not a small hole in the ground but the mouth of a cave often large enough to emit such a copious flow of water that it forms a navigable river.

Such springs are commonly found in Florida, particularly through the midsection of the state adjoining the Suwannee River. Of the hundreds of Florida springs of all sizes, twenty-two are of major magnitude with an average discharge rate of at least 100 cubic feet per second, making each of them capable of providing water for a city of 500,000 people. Two of these major springs put out sufficient water to supply cities of over three million people.

As divers, we were interested not so much in the quantity of a spring's flow as in its quality: how clear it was for exploring the internal cave system. A local rain or a backed-up river system, for example, could turn normally clear spring water the color of milk, or worse.

No matter how large or small a spring cave system, they were all formed in the same manner. Where they are most common in the state, heavy underlying stratas of limestone came close to the surface. Over many centuries, rainwater percolating down through fissures in these deposits eroded away the softer portions and created mazes of subterranean tunnels, sometimes honeycombing the limestone and other times sculpting it into surrealistic filigreed forms. Sometimes surface waters collecting in dish-shaped limestone pools eroded through their bottoms until they caved in on even more heavily eroded caverns, creating a so-called sinkhole formation, at times with a characteristic hour-glass configuration similar to Little Salt and Warm Mineral springs.

For some divers what was more enticing than just the challenge of exploring these sunken mazes was the thought that perhaps once upon a time, between fluctuating sea levels, the caves were inhabited by prehistoric animals, or early humans, or perhaps even used to conceal treasure. No more stimulus than this curiosity was needed to make divers risk their lives to find out what was hidden in the caves.

In the late 1950s my fellow divers and I were well into the exploratory phase of cave diving, searching out and investigating every underwater hole in the ground that we heard about. And since scuba equipment had been available in the United States for only a few years, these areas were virtually unexplored. The drive to learn what these hidden rooms had concealed from prehistoric times to the present was enormous. For Florida scuba divers it was an era of unparalleled underwater exploration. Anyone with a face mask, swim fins and an air tank had the basic equipment to explore a world as ageless and unknown as the backside of the moon. Such people as Garry Salsman, Wally Jenkins, Henry Doll and other young college students were diving to depths of over 200 feet in Florida's giant Wakulla Springs near Tallahassee to explore 2,000 feet of the underwater cavern with its hundred-foot-high ceilings, "Grand Canyons" and remarkable fossil boneyard from which they salvaged a complete mastodon for the Florida Geological Survey. In the hope of perhaps making similar fossil finds, a few of us decided to make a trip to a cave near Brooksville,

Florida, called Sabertooth Cavern. Having heard that sometime in the recent past the complete skeleton of a sabertooth tiger had been found there, we wondered what else it might contain.

The underground system was both wet and dry, a dry cavern with a small pool at one end of it. To our knowledge no one had ever dived in the pool, and that was what interested us. What lay beneath those still waters? More sabertooth tiger bones? Or perhaps those of his victims? No one really knew unless he had been there.

Our group this time consisted of Charlie Carneal, Bob Chapman, Larry Jerome, Luanna Pettay and myself. Since this was to be strictly an exploratory trip, we carried only one tank and regulator.

After a rather difficult time finding the place, we were cautioned by people in the area that the cavern was dangerous because blasting was taking place not far away and they were afraid of a possible cave-in. We too were aware of this possibility because as we scrambled down the sloping main shaft of the cave we heard the distant rumble of blasting in progress. Once inside, however, we saw no significant rock falls from the ceiling and assumed it would be safe.

With our handlights probing the damp rocky walls around us, we moved down the sloping tunnel into the cavern for about 100 feet, finally reaching the floor of the main chamber. The glassy surface of the dark pool at one end of the chamber reflected our lights eerily into the dark walls above. The pool appeared to extend back about fifty feet under the sloping overhang.

Putting on mask and flippers, I got into the water to check it out. Once I looked beneath the surface I was surprised to see the bottom only five feet down, so shallow that we could walk across it. But in the distance, under a ledge, was an underwater opening into a much larger cavern.

Diving into the mouth of it, I shined my light about. The water was crystal clear and I could see over 100 feet in all directions.

Returning to the surface, I told the others what I had seen. "It looks like a big hole down there, probably well over 100 feet deep. It's about 125 feet straight across."

"Great," said Charlie, an avid cave explorer. "How do you want to attack it?"

"I'll put on a tank and take a line straight across to see what I can see."

"I don't much like the idea of you going into that place alone," said Luanna. "It doesn't seem too safe to me."

"Don't worry," I said. "As long as I have the rope I'll always have a way back. I certainly don't intend to lose that. You can pay it out as I swim."

"Okay, just be careful," said Bob Chapman.

I put on the tank, passed a loop of the line over my shoulders and eased into the pool. After taking a compass bearing I planned to swim due west as far as the line would reach.

As the others let out the rope I eased down through the black hole into the main cavern below. Staying close to the roof of the room, I moved forward slowly, sweeping the beam of my light in all directions.

After about fifty feet my light suddenly reflected off an undulating mirrored surface overhead. I recognized it as the underside of an air pocket about ten or fifteen feet long.

Slowly I ascended toward it with my hand overhead in case the pocket was so shallow that my head would meet rock instead of air when I went through that silver surface. But my hand touched no obstacle and I shortly followed with the light, which illuminated an air pocket about six or eight feet high. I took my regulator out of my mouth and sampled the air. It seemed all right so I made a mental note where the pocket was in case I needed it later.

Ducking under again I continued swimming along the roof in a westerly direction. Fifty to seventy feet farther I noticed the bottom of the cavern beneath me began sloping up and there were signs of another air pocket overhead.

I surfaced in a large cavern twenty feet high and extending as far as my light would reach. The air was foul. My light soon illuminated the reason—a huge hill of bat guano twelve to fifteen feet high piled in front of me. From the ceiling of the cavern overhead hung great black masses of bats. Seeing them in this pitch black hole surrounded by water surprised me; I knew that unless they were a special breed they could not swim underwater, so the bats must have found some other entrance to the cavern.

At this point, close to the end of my rope, I decided to return and tell the others what I had seen.

When they heard what I had found they were quite excited.

"What say we all swim back and see what's in there?" I suggested.

"How are we going to do that with just one regulator?" asked Luanna.

"I'll take you one at a time. Whoever goes can wear the tank and regulator. Halfway there we can surface for a breath in the air pocket, then go on."

Everyone thought it was a great idea. Charlie Carneal was the first to go. He put on the tank, I grabbed a breath and the two of us swam together to the air pocket, where we surfaced. I took another breath and we continued on to the next chamber and the pile of bat guano.

Leaving Charlie and his light there, I returned with the tank for Luanna. Despite the problems she often had scuba diving, she was anxious to see this hidden room for herself. I admired her courage. It was an eerie trip to the chamber, and it was even eerier once you were there. But Luanna's curiosity apparently overcame her fear and she had no problem whatsoever. After that came Jerome.

Bob Chapman elected to stay in the first dry cave for safety precautions. If some unforeseeable accident were to occur such as a sudden failure of our scuba gear, at least Chapman would be able to alert the outside world as to where we were.

Charlie and Jerome decided to explore as far back as they could in the bat cave while I took a look underwater. Luanna waited for me beside the pile of guano in total darkness.

The flooded cavern below appeared to be an old sink-hole in which the waters had eventually eroded away the floor of an underwater river and opened up this enormous chamber. I found no sabertooth tiger nor any bones in my search. Later when I surfaced and sat at the edge of the water beside the pile of bat guano I could distinctly hear the voices of Charlie and Jerome echoing hollowly from the depths of the cave. When they returned they said they had walked at least a mile, and although the passageway narrowed in places, they never came to its end.

Our return to the first dry chamber was made in the same way as we had come, until we were all back in the first dry room with Chapman.

It was a real pleasure to finally climb out of the dank underground cavern into the fresh air and bright sunlight outside. We'd found no sabertooth tigers but had enjoyed a unique adventure, spiced up a bit when we were later told by local townsmen that the bats in the cavern were rabid.

Our next trip took us to Ponce de León Spring near De Land, Florida, not in search of fossil bones this time but in search of Spanish treasure.

The spring is a dish-shaped pool about 150 feet wide and 30 feet deep with two small openings, one about a foot wide and the other about three feet wide. Through these holes rushes a river of water, some twenty million gallons a day.

Local legend says that some of Ponce de León's soldiers were ambushed here by Indians and to prevent the savages getting a chest of gold, the Spaniards tossed it into the spring. According to the story the outflowing currents of the spring were so strong that no one was ever able to dive down through them and retrieve the chest of gold. Suffice to say this was the kind of story that whetted our appetite to dive Ponce de León Spring.

This time our group consisted of Charlie Carneal, Ken Henne, Ken Howe and myself. As we put on our double-tank Aqualungs and swam down to the mouth of the spring, it became apparent why no one had been able to breach that current to get the treasure. The column of water gushed through the narrow cave mouths with such force that every effort we made to cling to the jagged rocks around the main opening was unsuccessful. The currents blew us up into the pool like leaves caught in a whirlwind.

We tried tying a twenty-five-pound weight on the end of a line and tossing it down into the hole. The current tossed it right back at us. Next we tied a 120-pound weight on the end of the line and tried that. This worked better, except as the weight tumbled around near the opening it stirred up enough silt to blind us. Finally we managed to get the weight through the main hole and pulled ourselves down the line into the cave.

Once inside we flattened ourselves against the wall to avoid the main outrushing torrents of the spring. This was great, except that a quick check of our air supply revealed that with all the exertion we'd used up half our air. I gave the others the high sign and we rode up that one-way liquid escalator back to the surface to discuss our next strategy.

Before making a deep penetration into the cave we knew we had to have more air. This meant a trip back to town for refills. Then, once in the main part of the cave, we would tie a rope to our heavy weight and use it as a guideline, paying it out as we explored our way into the tunnels.

First though, since we had gotten this far and I still had thirty minutes of air left, I wanted to take a quick look around inside the cave just in case that chest was sitting there waiting for someone to tie a rope to it and haul it out. Charlie Carneal said he would join me since he had about the same amount of air left.

The two of us started down the line into currents so powerful that they almost tore off our masks. We kept fighting our way until we finally reached the heavy weight and were able to move back out of the main flow of the current. I switched on my flashlight and looked around.

Wherever that chest was, it wasn't lying there where we could see it. The tunnel angled downward, continuing into the darkness.

Leaving the weight behind I swam a short way into the tunnel. It was dark where I was, but looking back I could see the dim light filtering down from the main exit; the way out.

I went a way further, moving my flashlight beam back and forth over the uneven floor of the cave. Suddenly the pale yellow beam picked out a rectangular object at the far end of the shaft.

Is that the chest? My heart skipped a beat. I had to see what it was.

I swam toward it. The closer I got the lighter colored it became. Then I recognized the object as a cement block with a long rope tied to it. The rope led off into the darkness. I touched it. It was loose. Pulling on it I brought in about a sixty-foot length.

Since I had the only light I looked back to see where Charlie Carneal was, but I couldn't see him. Nor did I see the dim light of the shaft opening. Apparently in following the floor there had been a slight bend in the shaft that put me out of sight of him. Lacking light, Charlie would have stayed back near the entrance.

I looked over the cement block, wondering how it had gotten there. Apparently we were not the first divers into the springs. Someone had used the block the same way we were using our heavy weight. It looked like the perfect setup for me to use to make short exploratory trips. All I had to do was let out line to explore the cave and then come back to the cement block.

I glanced at my depth gauge. It read fifty-five feet. I moved out along the dark passageway, paying out line as I went. I passed a tunnel on my left and then a ledge. A little later I entered a room whose sides fell away so far that I could no longer see them in the beam of my flashlight. About then I reached the end of my rope, and it slipped out of my hand.

I reached back for the rope and was unable to find it. I turned the light to where it should be on the floor. But there was no floor!

Suddenly I was completely disoriented. *Where the hell am I?* There were no longer any rock walls around me, just water.

No current and no rope.

I made a short circle around and found nothing. I was in a huge void of water. Finally I made up my mind as to which direction I had come and I went that way.

A minute later I found a rock wall. Another one appeared on my other side. *This must be the tunnel shaft I came down.*

What an enormous relief! I started following it and suddenly came to a dead end! My relief vanished, replaced by a gnawing fear. *Stay cool,* I told myself. *Don't panic. You're close to the way out, just keep your head.*

I turned around and started following the floor. Or was it the ceiling! I had no idea which it was because it suddenly stopped and I was back out in the void of water again, suspended over a black abyss. I looked down and in my light I could see for about seventy-five feet. The tunnel just kept going.

I turned the light overhead and thought I saw the tunnel going that way. But which way was I to go? I looked at my depth gauge again, shocked to see that it read ninety feet. At that depth my air would not last long.

I wasn't too sure that I was even oriented up and down. Watching my bubbles didn't tell me much either. But I knew a sure way to find out: I took off my weight belt and dropped it.

As soon as I saw which way it went I turned and started in the opposite direction, lighter now by ten pounds.

Before long I found myself in a tunnel about six feet wide. It dead-ended. I turned to go back and encountered another wall. *My God, I'm completely walled in!* Totally disoriented now, I couldn't see how it was possible that there wasn't some opening . . . or how I had even got in there. Then I found a hole just large enough for me to squeeze through.

On the other side was a large chamber. Once again I was confused as to which way was up and which down. I shined my light on my bubbles and they seemed to be standing still in the water. *This is crazy. I must be losing my mind!* I concentrated on watching them. This time they seemed to be streaming off toward my feet. I couldn't believe it. Was I turned upside down? Everything seemed topsy-turvy. But thinking that my bubbles must know something that I didn't, I flipped over and started following them in that direction.

All I found were pools of quivering air that looked like mercury shivering against a rock ceiling. The air had gone as far as it could and now was stopped by the ceiling. If it couldn't find a way through, neither could I.

About then I realized that my air was drawing harder, getting more difficult to breathe. I knew I was about ten minutes from the end of it . . . the end of everything. My mind raced. *Not much time left. If I don't find the way soon, I never will.*

Suddenly a familiar shape loomed ahead of me. A hump of rock I thought I recognized. *Haven't I passed it about three times? Careful, careful . . . your fins are stirring up sediment. You won't be able to see a thing!*

I stared at the particles hanging still in the water. Not a sign of a current. *Lord, where is that current? Where is it when I need it most? If I had just the slightest inkling of which way it was going I could follow it.*

I moved off in a hopeful direction and came to another dead end. *How many is that, for crying out loud?* I turned and swam in another direction, my movements more urgent now, trying to hold down my breathing while my heart raced and I fought the terrible urgency to pant, to suck up hard the last life-giving air like a drowning man savoring the last few sweet lungfuls. I couldn't have more than a few minutes of air . . . of life. My God! I thought of my family, of my children. I thought how ashamed I was to let myself get into this situation. All I was doing was bumping around inside my own tomb. *God, I hope they'll never find my body.* I actually looked around for some place, some crevice, some insignificant niche to hide so that no one could ever find it and know of my stupidity.

Oh no, my light's going out! No, thank God it's just the silt, but it's very dim. I clicked it off, practically resigned that it was just a matter of minutes now. Even my breathing seemed to slow with that realization. I held each lungful as long as I could, savoring it to the last. I swam slowly through the darkness . . . ten or twelve kicks, then I ran head-on into a wall. My hand scrubbed over the rough surface until again I realized I was at a dead end.

Turning back in another direction I went on. Sometimes I stopped, suspended in the blackness, straining my eyes to see something in the darkness, praying to see just one small glimmer of light that would tell me *that* was the direction, *that* was the way out.

Suddenly I thought I heard a church bell ring loud and clear. Then I realized that I had drifted up and banged my tank against the ceiling.

I turned over and felt it, fly-walking along it upside down, struggling to find the highest point. I turned on the flashlight again. Its beam was so weak that all I could see was a few feet of the big black stone-walled coffin around me. Then the light winked out, completely and finally. I bumped into another wall and felt along it.

Suddenly my hand closed on a soft sinuous shape. *My God, a rope! It's a rope!* My heart surged. I pulled myself along it frantically. It seemed to take forever. Then abruptly it ended and I felt the cement block!

I was so close now. *But which way? Where's the opening?* I payed out the rope again, swimming around the block, straining my eyes to see light. My air came much harder now; I was close to the end.

I felt a slight tugging against my body. I stopped. It was the current! There was only one way that it was going: straight to the surface. I let go of the rope, concentrating on not moving a muscle, letting the current push me.

I moved faster, faster. *Where's the light? It can't be night!* Then I saw it.

Suddenly I was jammed head-first into an opening hardly big enough to admit my head. *The wrong hole! I'm in the wrong hole. The other one is here somewhere close-by.*

I clawed my way backward through the current that was pinning me to the opening, struggling back down into the shaft. If I was getting any air out of my regulator now it was a miracle. Everything looked hazy. But in that haze I saw the weight we'd dropped down the shaft. And then the blessed opening. *Thank God I can make it now!*

As I started through, something grabbed me by the neck and held me fast! The water surged around me.

Oh, no, no, no! I was caught on the limb of a dead tree that had wedged itself between my back and my tank, holding me tight to the bottom where the torrents rushed around me.

I can't get loose!

With my last remaining ounces of strength I struggled against this final barrier, the one thing that stood between me and life itself. Somehow I tore myself free and pushed up through that glorious long, swift rise back to the surface.

When my head shot out of the water I gasped a lungful of the sweetest air I'd ever tasted. Then I saw my friends splashing out to help me in . . . and at that moment I knew exactly what it felt like to be born again.

14

~~~~~~~~~~~~~ *the impossible find*

DR. EUGENIE CLARK felt certain that Warm Mineral Springs would prove to be just as productive as Little Salt Spring in our search for the remains of early humans. One day I took Genie and Luanna Pettay with me down to the ledge at thirty-five to forty-five feet, an area I had been working with some success. In one place we fanned our way down through four feet of sediment and found a crevice in the bedrock. Feeling along this crack I touched leaf deposits, and beneath them several small human bones. As we worked our way up the slope fanning sediments, we suddenly came to a piece of log. It was about eighteen inches in diameter, five feet long and three inches thick; the entire center had been burned out.

Carefully we fanned the sediments from the log, then the three of us surfaced and discussed what should be done next. Since this was more Luanna's field we decided that she should select a sample for carbon-14 dating. The three of us returned to the site and continued excavating under the log in the crevice.

Genie found several bones including part of a child's skull. Luanna found a human finger bone. Since the log appeared to be a particularly good specimen for dating because of its size and its association with the human remains, we brought it to the surface, where Luanna removed a good-size piece.

Genie contacted Dr. Carl L. Hubbs, a noted ichthyologist who had done work in paleontology and archaeology at Scripps Institution of Oceanography in California. She told him what we had found. Dr. Hubbs persuaded Dr. Suess at the Scripps Radiocarbon Laboratory to run a carbon dating on the sample we had selected. This was a tremendous breakthrough for us. Genie and I both felt that the C-14 date would show that the sample was at least 10,000 years old, but Luanna believed it would prove not more than 2,000 years old.

Since it would take considerable time for the radiocarbon test to be run, we contented ourselves with further exploration of the springs. I was anxious to locate the source of this exceptionally warm water, whose surface temperature was eighty-six degrees year-round no matter what the air temperature was. This meant that a large amount of quite warm water was pouring into the basin from the floor of the system. I finally decided to line up a couple of divers to see if we couldn't find that warm water source.

Howard Barefoot and Charlie Carneal agreed to make the dive with me. We had no idea what the exact depth of the spring was, or even where the deepest part was. A weighted line dropped down from the edge of the crater indicated it was about 165 to 170 feet on the north side. On the south side we got a depth of 125 feet. All the sediments seemed to slope down toward the north side, so we assumed that the hot water source of the springs would be there.

In making our dive, however, we didn't dive due north, but about thirty feet west of north. As we descended through the darkening waters I carried down a 250-foot line. Barefoot and Carneal followed about twenty feet behind me.

At about sixty-five feet down, after passing through what would be the narrowest part of the spring's hourglass shape, the walls of the cavern angled back at a forty-five degree angle and continued downward. At 180 feet down I turned and saw that the others were behind me. As I examined the sloping ceiling of the cavern wall I was following, I found something that I was never again able to locate—the base of a huge stalactite that had broken off. Brushing away the sediments I saw the exposed growth rings. The base was about five feet wide. From that diameter, the missing part of the stalactite would probably have been about eight feet long. This evidence would indicate that sometime in the past the springs were dry down to 180 feet below the present water level. Prior to this the deepest stalactite we'd found was eroded and decomposing at the eighty-foot depth. But since I was never again to find this one at 180 feet, I later could only assume that this section of the ceiling sloughed off into the bottom of the springs.

Not far from the stalactite I found a chamber in the ceiling about ten feet high and ten feet across. But I didn't have time to explore it then; I made note of its existence and continued on.

By the time I reached the bottom my flashlight was growing dim. I held it close to the dial of my depth gauge and saw that the hand of the gauge was against the pin at 250 feet. It had to be wrong. Looking up, I could see Barefoot and Carneal's light about thirty feet above me. They had planned to dive to 200 feet and wait for me.

I had now reached the section of the cavern where the water was considerably hotter than it had been in the upper levels of the spring, so I knew I was approaching the source.

Suddenly the lifeline was jerked out of my hand! I felt around for it but it was gone. By then my light had faded to such a faint glow that it was useless. I looked up to where the others had been and could not see them. Everything was pitch black. No light whatsoever penetrated from above.

I didn't panic, but I knew I was in a bad fix. Something must have happened to Barefoot and Carneal. For some reason they had either aborted the dive and gone up, or they were in trouble. At any rate they had to be somewhere above me. I decided that the first thing I should do was drop my weight belt to enable me to float up to the ceiling of the cavern.

As the weights slipped free I began to rise. I put my hands overhead to protect myself from the rock ceiling. If I ever hit that hole in the ceiling and went through it, I thought, I might never find my way out. And it was doubtful that anyone would ever find my body in there either.

Fortunately I missed the hole. As soon as I hit the ceiling I turned over and fly-walked up the slope until I had risen high enough to see a faint glow of daylight from the center of the spring above.

Barefoot and Carneal were on the surface waiting for me.

"What the devil happened?" I asked. "Why'd you grab the line away from me?"

"We had problems," said Carneal. Once we got ashore he explained what had happened. About the time they reached a depth of 200 feet, Barefoot suddenly let go of the lifeline and took off to one side. Carneal followed him and saw Barefoot trying to climb the cavern ceiling.

Carneal grabbed him and tried to pull him back to where he thought the lifeline was. Barefoot started flailing his arms and fighting him. Carneal realized that he had narcosis so bad that he didn't know what he was doing.

In the struggle Barefoot suddenly pulled Carneal's mouthpiece out of his mouth. Carneal pushed him away and managed to retrieve it. Then Barefoot grabbed Carneal's face mask and ripped it off.

Partially blinded now, all Carneal could do was move up the slope of the ceiling until he saw daylight. There he found the lifeline and came back to the surface. Quickly he got another mask from shore and was preparing to go down for Barefoot when Howard's head popped out of the water.

Barefoot didn't remember much about the struggle they had below, but he said that when he finally rose in the water his thoughts began to straighten out and he made his way to the surface without any more trouble. So went one of my many unsuccessful attempts to find the source of the springs.

Sometime later geologist Harold Kelly Brooks made his second trip to the springs. This time he wanted water samples from the bottom and I volunteered to get them for him.

How best to go about it? We couldn't use plastic gallon jugs because the pressure would flatten them before we were anywhere near the bottom. Therefore we decided to use gallon glass jugs, hoping the glass would be heavy enough to prevent them imploding before I got the samples.

When I took the jugs down to the bottom, in over 200 feet of water, I found it impossible to unscrew their caps due to the tremendous pressure. I could only secure a water sample at 100 feet. I tried to get one deeper, diving to 150 feet, but when I released the cap the water rushed in with a pressure of sixty-seven pounds per square inch and the jug imploded in my hands. I got a nasty cut on my arm, and that was the end of that.

One day I got a telephone call from the National Broadcasting Company. A man named John Light told me that Chet Huntley was interested in Warm Mineral Springs because of an article he had read in a New York newspaper. Light indicated that Huntley might do a special report on the springs and my underwater discoveries, and he wondered if he could come down to discuss the matter with me. "Do you have any bones you've found that you can show me?" he asked.

"I certainly do," I said. "I'll be glad to show you what I have. I've just been excavating an area that has many human bones, and there's a possibility that farther up this slope I might even find a skull."

Light said he would catch the next plane out and we could get together and see what could be arranged.

When he arrived I showed him some of the bones that we had taken from the springs. He seemed only mildly interested. Later I learned that he had been involved in other supposedly authentic finds in Florida—in one case it was a treasure find and he learned later that it had been set up for the cameras by the individuals who stood to gain from the publicity. But fortunately Light was a diver, and after I took him down and showed him some of the human bones protruding from the untouched sedimentary layers I was working, he came to the surface with a much different attitude. Indeed, he was quite excited.

"You know," he said, "at first I thought this thing was a fraud, like so many promotional schemes. Sometimes everything you read about Florida sounds as if it's been written by a PR man. I came down here to investigate the authenticity of this story for Huntley, and from what I've seen so far it looks pretty authentic to me."

Light immediately telephoned Huntley and told him what he had seen. Huntley asked Light to contact a young Navy lieutenant, Glenn Brewer, an excellent Navy underwater photographer. Shortly afterward Brewer arrived with a 35mm underwater camera, long extension cables and powerful underwater lights.

I had long discussions with Light and Brewer about what I had done in the springs and how I had tried unsuccessfully to interest professionals in the exploration. I told them that I often spent eight to ten hours a day underwater, taking enough air tanks down to last me. Brewer said, "That just can't be, Bill, it's against all diving rules. Doing things like that, you should be dead now. Anyone who stays down in sixty feet of water for more than an hour has to decompress."

"You may be right, Glenn," I said. "But it never bothered me at the time." The trouble came later.

Brewer just shook his head. In the 1950s we didn't have much accurate literature about decompression and the bends. I think the Navy divers were privy to most of this information. I had a set of Navy decompression tables but never paid much attention to them. There were days when I would spend six hours offshore in twenty to twenty-five feet of water searching for fossil shark teeth, them come home and make a deep dive to around 230 feet in the springs. Sometimes in the evening I noticed that I would get a red rash across my chest and arms, but I always suspected this was chafing from the many big, rough fossil shark teeth I often crammed inside my tee-shirt. I now realize that I probably had a mild case of decompression sickness from too much underwater exposure without adequate decompression. Of course, I suspect that on my daily deep dives into the springs I was probably decompressing without really being aware of it. Taking enough tanks of compressed air to last me for eight hours underwater, my first dive would be around the bottom at about 230 feet. Then slowly I'd work my way up, swimming around the circumference of the spring, stopping to investigate as I swam. I would then stop to work at sixty-five feet for a while and then at the forty-foot ledge. Then to the ten-foot level before coming out of the water. I realize now that even though I didn't have any severe symptoms of the bends back in the 1950s, the nitrogen was building up in my system from the long hours of deep diving I was doing. Eventually it resulted in aseptic bone necrosis* necessitating a complete hip replacement in 1971. Considering my diving routine, it's no wonder that Brewer was a little aghast when he heard about it.

I gave Light and Brewer all the background information I had about what had gone on before and all the troubles with Dr. Goggin. I recommended that we have an anthropologist or an archaeologist on hand when we made the film. Since Luanna Pettay had been involved in so much of the spring's early exploration, she was my choice to be in on all this. I told Light and Brewer, "It's important that we get across to the public the tremendous importance of this site. I don't think we can do it without some scientific authority with us in the film."

Light and Brewer mentioned this to Huntley, but he replied, "Well, who made the finds anyway?"

They told him that I had made most of them and that Pettay and Clark had acted as observers. Huntley insisted that he just wanted me in the film and that it was not necessary to involve the others.

---

*Medically termed dysbaric osteonecrosis, the disease often strikes divers going too deep and staying underwater too long. Tiny air bubbles block blood vessels in the bone, causing the areas to eventually die and collapse. The damage to hips, shoulders or limbs requires plastic or metal replacements.

I took Brewer and Light down for a swim around the springs. We made one deep dive to the silt cone in the center, then they were ready to do their film for the NBC news special.

They rented a 110-volt gasoline generator to power their underwater lights. The generator wasn't too reliable, often stalling or running out of gas, making the lights go out. We had to have good light because available light from the surface was not adequate for filming. Finally we solved the problem by getting a 500-foot electric cord and hooking the 1,000-watt lights to an electric outlet near shore.

Brewer hired one of my diving buddies, Ken Howe, to assist; Burton McNeeley, another friend, was granted permission to make a 16mm film for his own use.

On the first two days we filmed surface scenes and some underwater segments. On the third and final day they filmed the area where I had been finding human bones. Since I had already found arm and leg bones and portions of the spinal column, I surmised that I might find the rest of the skeleton in the same area.

I had found the bones behind a small stalactite lying on a ten-degree slope. Apparently they had slid down this slope against the stalactite. If my prediction was correct, I would find the rest of the skeleton farther up the slope.

Burton McNeeley and his assistant, a Mr. McCarthy, felt that nothing much more was going to be found, so they left with their film. They should have stayed one more day.

The lights and cameras were on me while I was working. Slowly I excavated up the slope, fanning the sediments out of the way. When I reached the area that I had not cleaned off before, the sediments were much heavier and I began to find loosely packed leaves. As I carefully removed these leaves and sediments I saw something that came as a surprise even though I had been halfway expecting it—I uncovered the dome of a human cranium. When I had it partially exposed, the camera ran out of film. Brewer and the others signaled for me to surface.

We went up as excited as children. "I can't believe it!" I said. "It looks in good condition. I think it'll be a whole skull." We could hardly wait to get down and find out exactly what we had.

Since I had only exposed the dome of the skull, everyone was excitedly wondering whether or not it would be complete.

Loading the huge 35mm movie camera seemed to take forever. It was a tremendous job necessitating removal of the heavy housing and the exposed film, reloading and reassembling the camera in the housing. Then back down we went.

Very slowly and carefully I fanned away the sediments from around the skull. I was especially careful because I knew many skeptics would see this excavation and I wanted to be sure that it was all on film so that in the future no one would question the validity of the find.

Finally I uncovered the whole thing. It was complete with even the jawbone in place. The cameraman motioned to me underwater that he wanted me to stop and surface so that he could talk to me.

Topside he said, "Bill, I want you to take the skull up in your hands very carefully, swim slowly toward the camera, turn it so that we can see it from several different angles, then slowly swim up to the surface with it."

"Fine," I said. I wished that Genie Clark was there with me for this momentous occasion. She had been diving with me just the day before and was photographed swimming in the spring. Genie had such confidence in my work, and was one of the few friends who believed in me. It would have been a big thrill for her to have witnessed this find.

I dived back down to the site and carefully lifted the skull into my left hand, leaving the lower mandible in place. Turning the skull on its side to inspect the base of it, I saw leaves and sediments embedded in the skull's foramen magnum, the hole through which the spinal cord attaches to the brain.

I moved toward the camera and they filmed the close-ups. Then I started for the surface with it.

As I went up I gently brushed the leaves and silt from the base of the skull. After cleaning it off I noticed something peculiar sticking out of the foramen magnum hole at the base. I touched it and it felt like soft, slimy soap. I thought to myself, "What the devil kind of sediment is this?"

I reached into the hole, pulled out some of the soft soaplike material and looked at it as it tumbled from the skull . . . *it was pieces of brain!* I couldn't believe my eyes. It simply couldn't be, not in a skull this old!

While I had probed into the hole and dribbled this peculiar material into the spring, the cameraman had filmed the whole thing. Now that I realized what the stuff was, I turned the skull over and clamped my hand over the base of it to prevent losing any more. I was appalled at the damage I had done. At least I hadn't cleaned the whole thing out—part of it was still left inside the cranium.

The minute Light and Brewer came out of the water I shouted to them, "You've got to look at this . . . I think I have something here that's unbelievable!"

We saw it, and still none of us could believe it. Light got on the phone to Chet Huntley and told him about finding the ancient skull with the brain material inside. Huntley couldn't believe it either. Then we called Dr. Eugenie Clark at her lab in Placida.

She said, "Bill, I've got a physician and three trained biologists at the lab with me. Keep it in a pail of Warm Mineral Springs water and bring it over immediately. Try not to lose any more of the material than you can." From the sound of her voice I knew Genie was as excited as we were about the find.

The physician, Genie and the three biologists looked at the material through the foramen magnum and all thought it looked like fresh brain tissue. The skull and its contents were then immersed in Formalin as the "brain" seemed to be disintegrating. I said, "It may look fresh to you but it's been underwater in Warm Mineral Springs for thousands of years. How do you explain that?"

There was no way to explain it. No one had any answer. And we still had received no results from the C-14 dating of the charred log taken from the same area.

After a couple of days the brain tissue turned from white to gray and the rounded convolutions became shrunken. Genie thought that perhaps we should have left it in the natural water of Warm Mineral Springs, which had already done such an excellent job of preserving it for these many centuries.

Genie's husband, Dr. Ilias Konstantinu, a Sarasota physician, sawed open the skull in his office and removed the remaining parts of the brain tissue that were still inside. Neurosurgeon Dr. Benjamin H. Sullivan, pathologist John S. Bracken and biochemist Isador Chamalin all examined the tissue. They concurred that the tissue samples appeared to be cerebellum and cerebrum. All the large recognizable fragments appeared to be cortex.*

In an effort to get as much official verification of the material as we could, Dr. K. P. Oakley of the British Museum of Natural History was sent a Kodachrome transparency of the skull and a sample of the brain tissue itself. Dr. Oakley wrote us, "One is left without any doubt whatever that the fragments in question are pieces of human brain." Dr. Oakley also mentioned other human brains that had been preserved, but thought that the brain from Warm Mineral Springs appeared to be the first instance where preservation was believed to have taken place in water, even though initially the brain may have been in a dry or damp environment.

The preservation could have occurred due to some antibiotic condition of the sediment or spring water of Warm Mineral Springs. Also, the fact that practically no oxygen exists in the water at that depth probably helped in the preservation.

Finding this skull with the brain fragments enclosed was the climax of the NBC News film. The photogra-

*Results of these examinations are documented in a paper Dr. Eugenie Clark and I wrote about the unique find for *American Antiquity*, Vol. 26, No. 2., 1960.

phers had planned spending at least two weeks on the film but realized that anything else they photographed would be anticlimactic.

Once again we were confronted by the same old nemesis: When the scientific community was confronted with this evidence, they were sure we had perpetrated a hoax since the find was made before a movie crew and their cameras. They said this was too coincidental to be credible. And yet, that is exactly the way it happened.

I felt sure that once the news about Warm Mineral Springs became known to the public, professional archaeologists would become interested enough to continue the research. But unfortunately the event created just the opposite response. NBC decided not to show this film until we received a carbon dating of our wood sample from Scripps Institution. This finally arrived three months later. Genie and I had estimated that the date would be close to 10,000 years. The actual dating by radiocarbon process of the log sample was 8000 B.C. (10,000 $\pm$ 200 years [B.P.] Before Present).

15

~~~~~~~~~~~~~ *site sans scientist*

MAYBE IT WAS understandable that scientists refused to believe what we had found. After all, it was unique. One could believe a radiocarbon date of 10,000 years for a log sample, but the finding of a human skull in the same sediment with a partially preserved brain intact was simply too much strain on scientific credibility. A 10,000-year-old brain, indeed!

Consequently, the whole thing was viewed with skepticism by the scientific community. It was suggested that Dr. Clark, an ichthyologist, forget about the bones in

Warm Mineral Springs and stick to studying fishes. We were criticized because no reputable archaeologist had made the find or was on hand when the find was made. It was thought that the whole thing had been concocted simply to promote the health spa at Warm Mineral Springs.

Nothing could have been further from the truth. Yet it would take another seventeen years before professional people in the field of anthropology and archaeology would ever believe this, and finally have the courage to examine the site and see the evidence for themselves.

Despite the adverse publicity we were receiving from so-called professionals in the field who apparently had neither the time nor the inclination to pursue the matter further, I felt we should continue our efforts to interest some reputable scientific authority. I could not help but believe that someone, somewhere in the United States with the proper qualifications would hear about our finds and at least make some small effort to personally check their authenticity.

The charred log taken from the same general area as the human remains had produced one of the best datings ever obtained by Scripps. While it is possible to date bone material, it is not considered as accurate as datings made from organic material found in the same locality. This charred log provided an extremely suitable item for dating. Due to the skepticism about finding the skull, Genie wanted also to have the actual bone dated—not the skull itself, but other human bones from the same skeleton.

Jacques Cousteau, a friend of Genie's, offered to date the material for us at a laboratory in Monaco. He said that he would process it and get a date as soon as possible. He wanted the skull itself, but in order to carbon-date material the sample is usually destroyed and we did not want to lose this unique reminder of what well might be the first American. Therefore we sent samples of the skeletal material taken in association with the skull. Unfortunately, Cousteau's promise of a prompt dating turned out to be a two-year wait.

Apparently the delay occurred because he was dissatisfied with the results. Meanwhile, however, Captain Glenn Brewer, the photographer who had helped take the movie for NBC, was in Monaco on a tour of duty with the U.S. Navy and was able to bring back the dating data for us from the laboratory. The bones that were found in association with the skull were from a skeleton dated between 7,140 and 7,580 years old. While not as old as we had hoped, the date compared favorably with the Scripp's dating of the charred log sample.*

Studies by anthropologists tell us that the skull is that of a female about nineteen years old and about sixty-six inches tall. It is surmised that she was either a sacrifice or that she fell into the pool when the water was about forty feet lower than at present.

Not long after finding the woman's remains we had a rather unusual experience. It started with a newspaper friend of mine, Bob Fellows, who was then a reporter for the Tampa *Tribune.* Fellows used to dive with me frequently in Warm Mineral Springs and had written many articles about our activities there. He did an especially

---

*C-14 datings on bones are not considered to be accurate by archaeologists. Current study of this skull indicates it is in the 10,000-year-old range.

good job because he had seen our underwater discoveries first-hand. Now Fellows arranged for the famous psychic, Peter Hurkos, to come to Warm Mineral Springs and examine the bones we had found. Hurkos was the psychic who offered his services to the noted attorney F. Lee Bailey in the Boston Strangler case. Hurkos and his party arrived shortly after the NBC film crew left. Since he had recently returned to the United States from the Netherlands, and spoke little English, we communicated through his manager and interpreter.

Hurkos felt my body and examined me closely. And then he began to describe what was underwater at Warm Mineral Springs. His description was uncanny. He told me exactly the way the caverns and stalactites were located below the surface. Then he proceeded to describe a ledge forty feet below the water level with caves going back thirty or forty feet under the ledge. Until then, very little excavation had been done and few bones had been found except in the area where the skull with the brain had been discovered. However, Hurkos told us that we would find burials way back in the caves he described. Up to this time I had never seen such caves as he mentioned, although it was possible to shine a light back through narrow crevices where there was too little clearance between the sediments and the ceilings of the caves to allow entry. But Hurkos predicted that sealed burials would be found in these caves.

When the famous psychic examined the skull that I had found with the brain inside, he stroked it with his fingertips, closed his eyes and predicted that the dating would be 13,000 years.

When we later learned the results of the C-14 dating

we knew that Hurkos was off almost 3,000 years. We did not have any dates that old as yet from any of our recoveries, but his predictions on the burials back in the caves may one day prove to be correct once sediments are removed and these areas can be examined more closely. Only time will tell.

Meanwhile, Dr. Genie Clark kept trying through her contacts with various scientists at different universities to interest a team in coming to Warm Mineral Springs to conduct an exploration under scientific conditions. Dr. Hubbs at Scripps had told her that Warm Mineral Springs was one of the most important archaeological sites in the United States if not in the Western Hemisphere, and urged her to cease any further excavation until the proper funding could be obtained. Naturally it was difficult to get scientists from California interested in a project in Florida, not only because of the distance involved but primarily because Dr. John Goggin, the foremost underwater archaeologist in the country at that time, had already ridiculed the finds to such an extent whenever he was asked to verify the significance of the early man remains in the springs. One such occasion took place during proceedings of the 16th Southeastern Archaeological Conference held in Macon, Georgia, in 1962. During the delivery of a talk on recent developments in underwater archaeology,* Dr. Goggin said, "A few miles from Little Salt Spring there is another one called Warm Mineral Springs in which I also made one brief dive down to about a hundred feet with Lieutenant

*Excerpted from "Recent Developments in Underwater Archaeology," John M. Goggin, Proceedings of the 16th Southeastern Archaeological Conference Newsletter, Vol. 8, May 1962, Macon, Georgia.

Colonel Royal, the man who had found the first bones in there. [*Dr. Goggin never dived with me in Warm Mineral Springs.—Royal*]

"Warm Mineral has an interesting history," Dr. Goggin continued. "It is also being developed by people who are selling lots around it. They sell bottled water from it and they let you bathe in there for a fee, all presumed to increase your laxativity. At the present time they are trying to convince the city that this is Ponce de León's fountain of youth. The operators of Warm Mineral Springs hired a very aggressive promoter who kept encouraging this Colonel Royal to dive here. So Colonel Royal, together with an ex-geologist named Dr. Eugenie Clark—a very famous shark expert who wrote the book *Lady with a Spear,* which you may have read—have been operating in Warm Mineral Springs. And as you probably know if you have been looking at television, they have made some very sensational discoveries all by themselves without any consultation with any archaeologist, and with only a slight consultation with Dr. Pettay . . . I do not know who did most of it—Royal did most of it, and apparently Dr. Clark got involved. They got a log and some other bones, including a skull with a brain intact. I heard about this from many sources. . . .

"The observations, as far as I know, were made in the water by Colonel Royal. I dove with him, and before I went down he explained to me what I would find in these springs. What I found was certainly different than he described. I have no faith in his powers of observation. . . .

"Their argument, of course, is that these things were deposited when the stalactites were being formed. If stalactites were being formed, it was a pretty wet period, and the idea of people being back in there in a little niche presents a problem. According to Colonel Royal and Dr. Pettay these niches are six feet, maybe, but not much more. From what I saw, six feet would be a pretty good measurement. It is a very fascinating problem, but this business of ichthyologists and retired Air Force officers setting themselves up as archaeologists is a little discouraging. . . ."

To me, the discouraging part was that egos and professionalism were apparently involved.

In our search for a qualified scientist we encountered more than one quack pretending to be an authority. We had a lengthy correspondence with one "scientist" from a research institute who seemed quite interested in our finds. I spent much time and effort sending him material for C-14 dating both from Little Salt and Warm Mineral Springs. He wrote back glowing scientific reports and urged me to send more. After numerous letters were exchanged with this gentleman, Genie Clark felt that something did not quite ring true about the man. She contacted the institute where he was supposedly employed and learned that he was a night watchman there who had access to stationery and scholarly texts with which he was able to carry on his impersonation of a knowledgeable scientist.

At Genie's urging I curtailed my excavations at the forty-five-foot level since it seemed to be of great archaeological importance, and decided to explore the two-foot to eight-foot ledge at sixty-five feet which seemed to almost completely encircle the springs. Below this ledge is an overhang of about five feet. While I never expected to find anything on this level, closer observation and a little fanning revealed to my amazement fossil animal bones that experts later identified as the bones of a giant ground sloth, a glyptodont (a five- to nine-foot armored relative of the armadillo), a cave bear, a horse, a smilodon (a saber-tooth tiger), and a few human bones. Most of these remains turned up under this overhanging ledge. Once again when I encountered the human bones I curtailed my activities.

After that I decided to go even deeper into the maw of the springs to try to determine just how far down these early remains could be found. My exploratory dives revealed numerous other ledges around the perimeter of the pool, all capable of containing fossil animal and early human remains to the bottom of the springs. It would take a team of archaeologists years to adequately investigate every one of these sites.

In one of my explorations I uncovered another almost perfect human skull embedded in a clay deposit. This deposit is much older than the leaf beds where I had found earlier skulls. Since these clay deposits were the only places where I had found ground sloth bones, I presumed that this skull was older than the ones I had found before. As soon as I found the skull I left it untouched *in situ* and discontinued my excavation of the area.

Again we encouraged professionals to look at the find. Dr. Eugenie Clark, who was still fanning the coals among her professional acquaintances, dived with me to examine the skull. Dr. Clark contacted Dr. Harry Shapiro, Curator of Anthropology at the American Museum of Natural History, who after examining bones from both springs felt that an investigation might prove rewarding.

He encouraged a colleague, Dr. Ford, to come to Florida to investigate the sedimentary layers. On his way to Warm Mineral Dr. Ford stopped off to speak with Dr. John Goggin in Gainesville. Dr. Goggin had repeatedly insisted that the human bones I had discovered had just drifted down through the sediment and were not in undisturbed layers of chronological age. Now Dr. Ford would have an opportunity to see whether or not this was true.

I was overjoyed to know that at long last some authority was going to take a look at the underwater site and see the situation for himself. Dr. Ford arrived and told us he had just one day to spend diving with us. As luck would have it, on the day we attempted to dive so that he could personally see that the bones were in naturally sedimented layers, Dr. Ford had a cold and could not clear his ears. The dive was aborted.

Once more we experienced frustration. We had no qualified anthropologist to evaluate our finds. All we could do was show Dr. Ford the movies that had been taken for NBC by Glenn Brewer and John Light. The doctor was enthusiastic about these films and really disappointed that he was unable to see the bones *in situ* and examine the site himself. From our experiences with diving scientists I was beginning to believe that sinus problems and colds were occupational diseases with them.

One interesting thing did develop as a result of my conversation with Dr. Ford. He told me before he left that Dr. John Goggin would like to have me come to Gainesville to settle our differences. I assured him that

I would be delighted to do so and certainly would make an appointment to see him in the very near future. Unfortunately, this meeting never took place. Circumstances required me to leave Florida shortly afterward and move to Texas for the next few years. During that time Dr. Goggin died.

Realizing that I would soon leave Florida, I tried once more to encourage a diving anthropologist to examine the latest skull that I had found *in situ.* If the skull wasn't removed, it would be stolen by unauthorized divers. But Genie and I finally had to admit that we had explored all possible avenues for getting a scientist to come look at the skull. In the end we had no choice but to remove it to a safe place.

Many years later, when a qualified anthropologist had an opportunity to examine this skull and the one containing the human brain, he felt that it was some of the earliest evidence of early man in the Western Hemisphere. The skulls are presently at Arizona State University in Tempe, where casts have been made of them for anthropologists to study in their pursuit of knowledge about America's earliest inhabitants.

After living and working in Texas for several years I returned to Florida in 1969. Just prior to my return I visited Dr. Marie Wormington, then Curator of Archaeology at the Denver Museum of Natural History and author of *Ancient Man in North America.* Dr. Wormington, who is now adjunct professor of anthropology at Colorado College in Denver, asked me why someone didn't start exploring at Warm Mineral Springs. She felt that it would prove to be a most significant site in the history of early man in America. She knew of the article

Dr. Clark and I had authored in *American Antiquity,* describing the skull with the brain that I had found in 1959, and she felt that Dr. Luanna Pettay would be the most likely person to write it up. I told her what had already ensued regarding our effort to locate adequate professionals and said that I had finally decided to go back to Warm Mineral Springs and do something significant there whether knowledgeable authorities were working with me or not. Too many years had been allowed to elapse while we tried to interest scientists in the find. Now someone had to do something positive whether on a scientific basis or not.

When I reached Florida, one of the first persons I went to see was Dr. Charles Fairbanks, who had replaced Dr. Goggin at the University of Florida after Goggin's death. Although I felt that Dr. Fairbanks might already be prejudiced against Warm Mineral Springs from what he had heard from Dr. Goggin, I still believed the University of Florida's Department of Anthropology was the proper place to take my information and to seek help once more.

Dr. Fairbanks appeared interested in what we had done at Warm Mineral Springs. On that basis I gathered all the material and bones that we had taken and labeled from both Little Salt and Warm Mineral Springs in the late 1950s and turned them over to him. He assured me he would examine the material.

Since I was anxious that some kind of work continue at the springs, I asked Dr. Fairbanks if it would be possible for the university to supply me with a compressor and diving equipment in exchange for whatever information or finds I could gather for them from the springs. The offer was declined.

I then went to Warm Mineral Springs and had a long talk with Mr. and Mrs. Fred Daley, Sr., owners of the springs. I said, "If you can furnish me with diving equipment, underwater camera and lights so I can continue exploration of the springs, I feel sure that I can put Warm Mineral Springs on the map as one of the most important archaeological sites in the world."

I asked for no pay whatsoever. My retirement plus Social Security would keep me in food and lodging.

The Daleys welcomed the idea. "It sounds like a reasonable arrangement, Bill. We believe you can do it." They agreed to supply me with whatever I needed for the project in the hope that my continued work would eventually attract the professional people the exploration required.

In the spring of 1970 I moved permanently to Florida, rented a small house at North Port near Warm Mineral Springs and began accumulating the equipment I needed for the job. Checking with my good friend Tom McQuarrie in Crystal River, I explained what I was about to do and he advised me on the best equipment to buy. Tom was rebuilding surplus military compressors and I purchased a Joy compressor with a fifteen-horsepower three-phase motor to use for filling my scuba tanks. After transporting this to Warm Mineral Springs I installed it in a shed I built for the purpose complete with the necessary wiring. I then purchased scuba tanks and other diving equipment and was ready for business.

From that moment on I began daily logging my time and discoveries on yellow legal pads. My first goal in the springs was to make an accurate diagram of the entire pool, recording depths, ledges, anomalies and other observations.

Through that summer of 1970 I spent many hours just swimming around at various depths fanning sediments that had been deposited over thousands of years. Most of my diving was done alone, and I spent from three to four hours a day at it. On May 20 I made a dive with Iris Woolcock, a remarkable lady who was then in her seventies. Iris dived with me to a depth of 100 feet, helping me place guidelines to this depth. While I was attaching a line to a stalactite I dislodged a heavy piece of tufa growth (a porous limestone formation deposited by the highly mineralized water on the stalactites). When it hit me I saw stars for a few moments, but fortunately it didn't knock me out.

The next day I dived to fifty feet to work areas I had begun in the 1950s. As usual I always took extra tanks down to enable me to stay longer. When I ran out of air at forty feet one day I attempted to change over to my auxiliary tank, but the valve on the second tank was so tight I wasted precious moments trying to open it. My regulator mouthpiece was out of my mouth and I was holding my breath. While having difficulty I muttered, "Dammit," and got a big mouthful of sulfur water for my trouble. That night and the next day I was down with diarrhea, probably from the dose of laxative water I had swallowed.

To make up for my day off I used up an additional three tanks of air the next day. In changing tanks I accidentally knocked off my mask and couldn't see to find my mouthpiece. Consequently I had to surface from fifty feet to get another mask.

Each day I dived revealed new vistas of the spring that I had never noticed before. I became so engrossed with my underwater activities that I would forget to come up and eat lunch. Someone solved this problem by giving me some Pillsbury Space Sticks, which I could stick inside my shirt and munch on if I got hungry underwater. With a little practice, eating underwater is no problem.

I installed an underwater light using a 500-foot cable given me by the NBC camera crew in 1959. This light, equipped with a 1,000-watt bulb, enabled me to see way back into the cave.

Each day's dive resulted in my uncovering large numbers of fossil bones from prehistoric animals that had either fallen into the springs or been driven there to be butchered for food. Mixed in among these animal bones were scattered human bones.

A good friend and daily visitor to the spa, Dr. Rudy Splavec, gave me a copy of the excellent *Atlas of Human Anatomy*, which served as a fine reference for identifying the human bones.

Just the geology of the spring provided unlimited hours of investigation. From fifteen feet below the surface at various levels down to a depth of eighty-five feet I found both stalactites and stalagmites, the former still hanging from the undersides of the ledges. Many had fallen from the cavern ceilings above in ages past. Some of the fallen stalactites lying on the ledges below were fifteen feet wide, ten feet long and five feet thick. If the theory of stalactite growth of one inch every century is valid, those stalactites must have taken around 12,000 years to form. Where they were broken I saw growth rings similar to those in a tree that were thick in some places and thin in others, indicating wetter or drier periods when more or less water percolated through these formations. Between these rings were various colored deposits and often layers of tufa growth indicating periods when the stalactites were submerged, for the tufa deposits only form underwater in a supersaturated solution of the highly mineralized spring water.

These rings and the various kinds of deposits within them indicated that the springs had been both above and below sea level several times during the past thousands of years. Stalactites formed below eighty feet were badly decomposed. Geologists told me that this erosion was caused by fresh water eating away the limestone. This indicated that in the springs' history there were probably several freshwater "invasions," times when the water became sweet and drinkable but destructive to the limestone formations. One fallen stalactite I found was embedded in the bedrock, which appeared to have formed around it. Since a stalactite falling from the ceiling above onto this hard dolomite sandstone would have shattered to bits, how did this one become embedded in this fifteen- to twenty-million-year-old Miocene formation? It was a mystery to me.

Most of the summer was spent surveying, taking measurements and setting lines from sixteen points around the underwater circumference of the spring. These were safety lines that would enable me to find any point with the least amount of difficulty. Often while I decompressed I would excavate small areas in shallower depths, always finding a wealth of human and animal bones wherever I fanned away the sediments.

In early September 1970 it was my great fortune to meet Doris "Dottie" Davis, an employee of the Sarasota County Historical Commission. Doris told me that she knew about my early exploits at Warm Mineral Springs and she had been trying to locate me for several years. The Sarasota County Historical Commission was formed for the purpose of preserving historical artifacts and information within the county. I told her about what I had seen underwater, but it was difficult to describe something like this to someone who had never been in water over her head. I promptly decided that this lady had to learn to dive so she could see for herself what existed in our unique "underwater museum."

Dottie was an apt student and was soon able to dive down with me to see and photograph the site for herself. In her capacity with the Historical Commission, Dottie contacted the Florida Department of Archives, History and Records Management in Tallahassee and told them about my finds at Warm Mineral Springs. Unknown to me, this department had been organized while I was in Texas. One of its primary functions was to oversee the recovery of historical artifacts and treasure from Spanish shipwrecks being worked by treasure salvagers under contract to the state. Dottie received word that the state underwater archaeologist, Carl J. Clausen, was indeed interested in the finds in Little Salt and Warm Mineral Springs and would come down to examine the sites for possible future archaeological work.

I was tremendously pleased at this response and felt that at long last we were about to get the break we had been working for.

Meanwhile, while we awaited Clausen's arrival, I decided to lift a number of the stalactites lying on the ledges underwater to make a display on the grounds where everyone could enjoy them.

With the help of Ray Emrick, the head gardener, we

lifted some of the stalactites from the upper ledges of the spring. I would tie one end of a long rope to a stalactite, bring up the line and tie the other end to Emrick's tractor. Then he hauled the formation up out of the water and moved it into position for display. Other stalactites deeper in the springs we had to bring up with the help of numerous diving companions including Charlie Patton, Tiny Wirs, D. G. and June Mitchum, Jim Smith, George Wheeler III, Les Koher and his son Ed, Dick and Marion Almy, Pat Carter, Mike Straube, Dottie Davis and my present wife Shirley.

All of these divers worked many hours diving down to the ledges, tying ropes around these huge monoliths and then using fifty-five-gallon drums to lift the huge loads to the surface. One end of the drums was cut out, and after sinking them to the proper depth we roped them to the stalactites. Air injected into the barrels from our regulators displaced the water inside until they lifted their heavy burdens to the surface. Sometimes we accidentally overfilled the drums with air, causing them to rocket to the surface and fly halfway out of the water in an effort to become airborne. Rigging faucets on the barrels and bleeding off the expanding air as the units rose enabled us to control the ascents.

Every dive into the spring was like a trip back into time. The underwater cavern was a gigantic liquid-filled time capsule containing secrets that had been hidden there for thousands of years. Removing these broken stalactites and stalagmites from the ledges uncovered more of this past—numbers of bones both human and animal that I left untouched. Their presence only adds to the mystery. When we raised one large slab of rock that had apparently fallen from the cavern roof or wall, I discovered a pile of hard-packed leaves with a human femur on top of the vegetation but underneath the rock slab. Near the bone, six inches deep in the leaves, I uncovered a spearpoint in beautiful condition. Since this was the first point I had ever found in Warm Mineral Springs, I was excited. I continued searching in the same leaf bed and within the next two days found two more points, one of them an arrowhead made of the same kind of flint. So far as I know these are the only pieces of flint ever found in Warm Mineral Springs.

One day on the north side of the pool in thirty feet of water I started fanning away sediments from a sixteen-foot-long ridge. It soon became a triangular-shaped rock that had apparently sloughed off the wall from above. Excavating down one side of it to a depth of six feet, I encountered leaf beds from which I uncovered two finely worked pieces of deer antler. Under the leaves I reached what I thought was bedrock. But I soon found it too was another large rock that had fallen from above and split open, creating a five-foot-wide fissure twelve feet deep that narrowed to a foot wide at the base. The long triangular rock from above had fallen atop the break and formed its roof. However, before this occurred the deep fissure had filled with claylike sediments, packed leaves and broken stalactites. In excavating it, all I found was half of a human jawbone, which I left untouched. But around the triangular cap rock I discovered several worked bone needles and, not far from these, a large broken fossil shark tooth whose edge appeared to have been chipped for use as a cutting or scraping tool. Later I viewed these finds under a magnifying glass and noted striations on the bone needles which could have been caused by the uneven edge of the sharktooth tool. I had no trouble envisioning early man sitting astride this large triangular rock when it was above water, carefully using the fossil sharktooth to fashion the artifacts I had just found.

The crevice under the cap rock intrigued me. Although the supporting rock was badly eroded by fresh water, I felt that if I could excavate far enough back into this crack I could find something significant. Consequently I spent many days beneath this huge rock excavating sediments. One day while I was far back into the crevice a strange feeling came over me. Something told me to get out from under there at once. Not one to argue with intuition, I backed out of the hole as quickly as I could.

As I hovered in the water, looking at the dark opening and feeling foolish for letting my imagination get the best of me, I heard a muffled crunch. Before my startled eyes the whole thing caved in!

It scared the daylights out of me. To this day I don't know what told me to get out of there at that particular moment, but I'm thankful that I did. Had it caved in while I was under the rock no one would have known what ever happened to me.

On another occasion while working by myself at sixty-five feet, the silence of my underwater world was broken by the strangest sound. I first heard "Glugggg, glugggg, glugggg," similar to the sound of air gurgling out of a jug that has been thrust underwater. I listened carefully, trying to identify the deep, eerie gurgle. Again it came, "Glugggg, glugggg, glugggg," louder this time. Ceasing work, I swam to the surface to find out what it was. Almost at once I was confronted by a panicky bather who shouted, "My friend was swimming behind me across the pool and when I looked back he was gone! Please help me find him!"

Immediately I dove down and searched the pool to the 140-foot depth. But since I had already been underwater five hours I had used up all my bottom time and could stay no longer that day without risking the bends. Surfacing, I phoned a professional salvage diver friend, Tiny Wirs, and asked him to help search. Tiny hurried over with his diving gear and on his second trip down he found the body and brought it up. The man apparently suffered a heart attack while swimming across the pool. The eerie sound I heard was air being squeezed out of his body by the water pressure as he sank into the depths, a sound I hope never to hear again.

16

~~~~~~~~~~~~~~~ *ordeal by water*

IN THE SEPTEMBER 1970 issue of *National Geographic* magazine I read an article by Dr. George J. Benjamin entitled "Diving into the Blue Holes of the Bahamas." Dr. Benjamin described diving through underwater caves at Andros Island and told about finding and photographing the first stalactites ever discovered in a saltwater cave (the depth was over 100 feet). This information intrigued me, especially since the article mentioned that the blue holes were formed most probably as dry land caves or sinkholes during previous Ice Ages. I immediately wrote to the *National Geographic* requesting Dr. Benjamin's address, and they forwarded the letter to him in Toronto, Canada.

A research chemist whose avocation is underwater exploration and photography, Dr. Benjamin wrote back that he was interested in our investigation at Warm Mineral Springs but that he had no time to undertake a similar investigation. Instead he suggested that I contact Francis Kohout, a hydrologist with the United States Geological Survey in Washington, D.C.

I immediately got off a letter to Mr. Kohout, inviting him to visit and to dive at Warm Mineral Springs. He accepted. Shortly afterward, Kohout, Dr. Deric O'Bryan who was an archaeologist for the Geological Survey, and professional diver Bob Hill from Merritt Island, Florida, arrived to spend a couple of days diving and taking water samples in the spring.

This was the beginning of a long and enjoyable friendship with these men, especially Fran Kohout, who wanted to study the water that was coming into the springs at its deepest point.

After making numerous tests and collecting a number of samples, Kohout told me that he believed the source of the water came from what he called the Boulder Zone. It seemed that oil well drillers throughout most of southern Florida found that when they drilled down to depths between 2,500 and 3,500 feet, they found caverns that were often up to ninety feet deep. When their drills broke through into these deep subterranean recesses, knocking off large rocks and boulders from the ceilings, the drill bits would bound around in the boulders and often break off. Each time the well drillers hit these areas, a head of about twelve feet of hot salt water, ranging from 108° to 112°, gushed up out of the drill holes.

Fran was interested in this water. He theorized that deep waters of the Gulf of Mexico or the Florida Straits seeped into the Boulder Zone and in turn were heated by the earth's pressure. After testing water samples from Warm Mineral Springs, he felt the springs was a natural outlet for Boulder Zone water.

Dr. O'Bryan took a sample of hard-packed leaves from the area where state archaeologist Carl Clausen was later to find and remove a human femur in early 1971. Dr. O'Bryan took his sample back to Washington, where it was radiocarbon dated and found to be 10,300 years B.P. (Before the Present).

Kohout subsequently provided us with a vaṣt amount of information about the springs' hot-water source, its mineral content and the age of the water coming from the Boulder Zone. According to hydrologists, the water is 10,000 years old, which concurs with our other evidence dating the site.

A frequent chore I performed at the springs was to catch any alligators that chanced to wander into the pool during cold weather. Since the spring water was a constant 86° no matter how cold the air got, alligators often traveled long distances overland to get into that nice heated water. Their presence scared the devil out of the cash-paying customers. Consequently, the management asked me to get rid of the gators for them.

The trick in capturing alligators by hand is to get behind their heads and keep away from their powerful tails. Then all you have to do is grab them around their middles and hang on. Once this was accomplished I would tie a rope around them and drag them to the beach area. Rangers from nearby Myakka State Park would pick them up and release them in more remote areas where they would bother no one.

In January 1971 Carl Clausen, the state underwater archaeologist, arrived with another state diver, Alan Dorian, to make a preliminary investigation of Warm Mineral Springs. It was a memorable occasion, for this was the first time in the history of Warm Mineral Springs that we had a trained archaeologist who could actually dive down and see the site for himself.

Clausen spent the better part of a week with us, and while he was here he brought up a human femur from the area where the Geological Survey archaeologist had taken the core sample that had carbon dated to 10,300 B.P.

Anticipating that there would be future archaeological work undertaken by the state in the springs, I ceased excavating and renewed my efforts to establish underwater guidelines to the most important sites so that when the scientists came in force with their diving teams they would be readily able to find their way to these important areas.

Eventually, after many repeated efforts through the years to locate it, fellow diver Tiny Wirs and I finally found what we felt was the warm water source of the springs. It was an opening on the north side of the basin at a depth of 230 feet. The water flowing out of this crack had temperatures varying between 90° and 92° F.

That January Francis Kohout returned to Warm Mineral Springs with a group of hydrologists and geologists to explore it further and to collect more water samples.

Drs. Jerry Leenhweer and Ron Malcolm from the United States Geological Survey in Denver, Colorado, John Stamer from the U.S.G.S. in Tampa, Florida, and Dr. Hal Henry of the geology department at the University of Alabama in Tuscaloosa spent two days with us. Bob Hill also joined the group to help us gather water samples.

Kohout, who had just recently learned to dive, was able to accompany Hill and me to 100 feet. At Kohout's suggestion I established sixteen lines from the surface of the springs to the bottom, with each numbered so that a diver could tell exactly where he was in the hole. We also set one of the lines down to the hot water inlet over 230 feet below, where a water sample we took proved to be half salt water, a factor that helped substantiate Kohout's theory of Boulder Zone water.

State underwater archaeologist Carl Clausen returned to the area and this time investigated Little Salt Spring, located on property now owned by the General Development Corporation, where I had dived in the late 1950s. Accompanying Clausen were divers Bob Vickery and Alan Dorian from the State Archives and History Department. Clausen evidently found enough evidence in Little Salt Spring to convince him that he wanted to undertake further studies there when financing was available.

In May 1971, with financial assistance from the General Development Corporation, the scientists began to set up installations at Little Salt that would enable them to begin their work.

Finally, that June, I corrected a problem that had been bothering me for years: my right hip had been causing me so much trouble that doctors told me an operation would be necessary. So I left for Abilene, Texas, to have it taken care of. After an examination at the Dyess Air Force Base Hospital, Dr. Peter Wirtz told me that I had aseptic bone necrosis necessitating replacement of part of the pelvic bone and femoral head. Dr. Wirtz felt this injury was caused by the constant diving I had been doing without sufficient decompression.

The operation took place on July 6, 1971. I drove back to Florida on July 20 and the next day, with the doctor's permission, I went diving in Warm Mineral Springs. Dr. Wirtz had told me that it was all right as long as I did not put too much weight on my newly installed femur.

Since I had been doing a lot of diving for fossil shark teeth off Venice Beach before the operation, I was anxious to continue to do so. Each day my wife, Shirley, would help me drag my ninety-cubic-foot double air tanks down to the water. We probably made quite a spectacle of ourselves: Shirley loaded down with mask, fins and a goody bag, dragging one side of the pair of tanks while I hobbled along on crutches dragging the other side. Once I got geared up and in the water everything was all right and I felt little discomfort. Shirley would take the crutches and return with them several hours later to meet me at the water's edge. At that time I was bringing in some beautiful shark teeth, many often five to six inches long; sometimes I would get twenty or thirty of them that were three and four inches long.

In the afternoons I would dive in Warm Mineral Springs to the tunnel entrance to clean out some of the sediments and enlarge the opening of the spring cave. Later, while decompressing at shallower depths, I spent many hours cleaning out the sediments between and under stalactites and stalagmites on the forty-five-foot level on the north side of the springs.

One day while doing this I found a perfect human lower mandible behind stalactites and under a big stalagmite. I left the jawbone where it was, thinking that perhaps the rest of the skeleton was nearby and might be buried in the surrounding sediments. Later I photographed the jawbone and the stalactites and stalagmites for the record.

Through the fall of 1971 I spent hundreds of hours diving to 230 feet daily, clearing out the sediments of the spring cave with a hayfork and photographing my progress. Unfortunately it was a slow process since at that depth I was able to work only about ten or twelve minutes a day before I had to come up for decompression. For this purpose I left extra tanks at strategic locations in the springs.

Although I sometimes had other divers with me, I generally worked alone at this depth. Most people were afraid of nitrogen narcosis or getting the bends. Primarily I wanted to enlarge the opening of this deep-water cave to where I could penetrate the tunnel and place numbered guidelines and floats at intervals. The shaft went back horizontally, reaching at one point a depth of 245 feet. The entrance consisted of a low ledge with an inverted "V" notch in it just large enough to allow a diver to squeeze through into the main tunnel.

On December 2, 1971, I attended a meeting at the Ramada Inn at Port Charlotte that signaled the start of the formal exploration of Little Salt Spring. Florida's Secretary of State Dick Stone and officials of General Development Corporation signed a contract enabling the state to continue exploration. All of the future work that was done in Little Salt was amply photographed and described by local newspapers and television. However, despite the fact that I was one of the original discoverers of the spring and had been instrumental in bringing in the State of Florida, I was not invited to dive during the project.

The following January, at the urging of Dottie Davis, Carl Clausen came over to Warm Mineral Springs to spend a few days. Before beginning his excavation, Clausen, accompanied by Bates Littlehales of *National Geographic* magazine and Gordon Watts, now state marine archaeologist for North Carolina, toured the springs with me to determine where he would excavate. I showed him all of the finds I had made that were *in situ,* including the mandible. I felt that the mandible should be excavated by Clausen, but he felt that removing all the stalactites and boulders would pose more of a problem than he had time to cope with.

Clausen and Watts did excavate an area about a meter square and secured samples of material, both zoological and botanical, for analysis and C-14 datings. In this meter of excavation he found bones of a six-year-old child, which when dated from wood samples in the same sediment level proved to be the oldest human bones ever dated from Warm Mineral Springs. They were 10,260 $\pm$ 190 years B.P. But Clausen's tenure in Florida was drawing to a close. Having already accepted a job with the State of Texas, he was preparing to leave in the near future for this new position.

After Clausen left Warm Mineral, Bates Littlehales stayed over a couple of days diving with me to photograph the mandible *in situ.* I explained to Littlehales the trouble I had had through the years and felt that his photographs might lend credence to my theories, and hence bring in a competent archaeologist to complete the job Carl Clausen had begun. I noted in my logbook that day: "Took photos of homo jaw. Found finger bones near jaw. Should prove to be a burial under limestone bedrock with stalactites over bones." My guess was soon to prove correct.

On March 16 I found a large Miocene bone lying on the floor of the tunnel, and another one embedded in the rock floor at the tunnel entrance. I had borrowed a 28mm lens for my Nikonos underwater camera from a friend, underwater pioneer Dimitri Rebikoff. A French engineer, Rebikoff is probably best known for his remarkable underwater diver propulsion units such as the *Pegasus,* and his later development of avant-garde underwater photographic equipment capable of performing feats never accomplished before. At this time, however, he had one of the first underwater-corrected 28mm lenses for the Nikonos and he loaned it to me to take pictures in the tunnel. The results were far superior to the normal 35mm lens I had been using on my camera.

On March 18 Rebikoff and his wife Ada were to fly to Venice in their private plane with their young assistant, Philip Levine, to dive at the springs. I wanted to return Rebikoff's lens to him, but first I needed to take some final pictures in the tunnel. The group was to arrive at Venice airport before noon. While Shirley went to meet them, I spent the morning and, as it turned out, a large part of the afternoon free diving with my daughter Moo-Moo and young George Wheeler down to fifty-foot depths. Since the Rebikoffs were late arriving, the two fifteen-year-olds and I did this from about 11 A.M. until 3 P.M.

When the Rebikoffs finally came they found they had forgotten their main movie camera and therefore were unable to follow their original dive plan to film in the springs. Meanwhile I had decided to go ahead and make the deep dive to take the photographs I wanted in the tunnel so that I could return the lens to Rebikoff.

Always when I made this type of deep dive my normal procedure was to carry a single seventy-two-cubic-foot tank under my arm while wearing a set of double ninety-cubic-foot tanks plus a twenty-four-cubic-foot pony tank attached to the doubles. All tanks except the pony were filled to 2,400 pounds per square inch pressure. I normally used the single seventy-two tank to go from the surface to the tunnel entrance, and would have about 1,200 pounds of air left in it when I reached bottom. Leaving this tank at the entrance, I would then start back into the tunnel with 2,400 psi in the doubles, plus the reserve in the pony tank.

After working in the tunnel taking photos, measurements and temperatures for not more than ten to twelve minutes at most, the air pressure would have dropped from 2,400 to 1,000 psi. At that depth I was breathing air at the rate of ten pounds psi with every breath, taking one breath every five seconds, using up 120 psi per minute. By the time I would get back to my single tank at the entrance, my decompression meter, which automatically computes decompression by simulating nitrogen absorption and elimination in the human body, would indicate that I should stop for my first decompression at fifteen to twenty feet. By the time I reached the sixty-five-foot ledge it would be reading another few feet.

Usually this combination of depth and bottom time required me to spend three minutes at thirty feet, six minutes at twenty feet and eighteen minutes at ten feet to breathe off the nitrogen in my system and avoid the bends. I always placed extra tanks at the thirty-foot ledge for emergency decompression, a safety measure I'd taken for over a year and never had to use.

On this particular day, however, the pattern changed. That was my undoing.

Because of the four extra divers that were arriving and planning to use my spare tanks, I dispensed with the emergency tanks at thirty feet, leaving all the others at the surface except one seventy-two-cubic-foot tank on the ten-foot ledge. I figured I could use the twenty-four-cubic-foot pony tank for my descent to the tunnel entrance, which would give me just enough air to get down there. With the double nineties for inside the tunnel, I thought this would be sufficient.

Before going down I plugged in the 1,000-watt light I had installed in the north tunnel on a previous day's dive. Things had already started going wrong, but I wasn't quite aware of it. I didn't feel right about making such a deep dive so late in the afternoon, but I decided to go ahead. It was about 3 P.M. when I started down, carrying the camera, two hand lights and the pony tank. Normally I always stay above my guideline so as not to stir up loose sediment, which rolls down the 35° slope toward the tunnel entrance and clouds the water.

Now, however, when I reached the end of the vertical descent line I ran into stirred-up sediment. Bad luck. I worked my way through the dark until I found the block of tufa near the entrance of the cave, where I placed my practically empty pony tank.

Looking toward the tunnel entrance, which was obscured by the cloud of sediment I stirred up when coming down the slope, I swam to where I thought the entrance was instead of following my guideline. For the first time in over a year of diving I went to the left of the entrance and missed it. About four minutes of precious air were wasted until I finally found it. At that time the thought occurred to me that I should abort the dive because everything was going wrong. But to Air Force pilots, abort is a dirty word. It means you have to cancel your mission due to failure along the line, usually some human error.

So I rationalized. Since this was to be just a quick bounce dive, I decided to go on into the tunnel, get the few photographs I needed and then get out—the whole thing over with in minutes.

Following my guideline under the tight "V" opening in the ledge and then back to where my 1,000-watt light had been, I discovered that the light was out. More bad luck. I took two quick photographs, looked at my pressure gauge and saw I had 1,000 pounds of air left, the amount I usually had when I would leave the tunnel and start my ascent. I thought to myself, "To hell with this. Everything's going wrong. I'm getting out of here!"

I started back along the guideline on the east side of the north tunnel. As I approached the area of the cave's entrance, which is always silted up by my passage into the tunnel, one of the worst things that could happen did. My lifeline broke through its rock mooring, and as I pulled it tight it slid into a narrow crevice under the rock ledge. When I followed it to the ledge, sediment boiled up around me, leaving me in total blackness. My handlight was useless. All I could do was feel along the ledge searching for the small V-shaped opening. I moved my hands over the rock trying to feel it. But all I felt in front of me was a solid rock wall.

I moved to my left. I knew it couldn't be more than twelve feet away but I couldn't find it. Finally I turned around and swam back, following the guideline into the tunnel. After going about ten feet I came out into clear water again. I was in the middle of the tunnel and could see my light cable and extra line along the west wall.

Following the line that had broken loose, I swam back toward the ledge and in total darkness tried again, still confident that I could find the small opening.

"It's *got* to be here. I've got to find it soon. My air isn't going to last much longer." But I simply couldn't find it.

Turning around, I went back into the clear water again. If I let go of the lifeline I knew I might go into a dead-end tunnel that was past the exit. At this stage of the game that would wipe me out for good.

I didn't even bother to take the time to look at my air pressure gauge because I knew I was already in serious trouble, even if I made it out all right. The next time I went into the clouds of silt I'd have to make it. My air was getting too low on my double tank. I tried to think what was the best thing to do. Finally I decided to grab my other lifeline and my light cord and drag them all to the left where the opening should be.

I moved way over to the left side of the tunnel and pulled all three of the cables together. Then I followed them into the sediments to the rock ledge. Finally I felt my body sliding through the V-shaped hole.

My doubles now were breathing hard. A few more feet . . . ten feet . . . and I would be in the clear. "Only hope is the pony tank . . . got to make it to the pony tank," I kept telling myself.

Finally I reached it. I remembered to exhale into it to blow out the sediment before sucking in. And then something tangled my light! I was caught fast! A slash of my knife cut it free. There was just enough air in my pony tank to let me make a dash for the surface. Even if I made it to my spare tank on the ten-foot ledge, I'd be lucky if I got out of this alive.

On my ascent, at about 120 feet, I started to belch through my mouthpiece, almost strangling as the rapidly expanding compressed air worked its way out of my lungs and stomach.

Coming up as fast as I could swim, I glanced at my decompression meter, which read close to forty feet. This should have been my first decompression stop to let me get rid of the nitrogen in solution in my bloodstream. I sure wished that I had my emergency tanks on the thirty-foot ledge.

At the sixty-five-foot level severe pains shot through my back and neck and under my rib cage. Pulling and swimming as fast as I could up the sloping line from the sixty-foot tieoff, I expected to see the other divers, Rebikoff and Levine, but there was no sign of them.

By the time I reached the ten-foot ledge and got to the mouthpiece of my spare tank, the air in my pony tank was completely gone. Ten seconds more and it would have been too late.

I went back down to the thirty-foot level to try to decompress, not daring to go deeper as I had to make the air last in the single tank until help arrived. The other divers should have been in the water by this time. My whole body felt like it was being pricked with needles. I had severe pains in my neck and ribs. The long haul to the surface without stopping to let the nitrogen out of my system was too much for my body to take. The nitrogen had now turned to gas and was bubbling through my bloodstream, trying to find a way out, and in doing so the bubbles were creating excruciating pain.

After waiting some thirty or forty minutes with no sign of any other divers, I knew I had to go to the surface to tell my wife that I was in trouble and needed double tanks for decompression.

I surfaced and shouted for help. Fortunately it came within minutes as Phil Levine quickly brought me my other tank. Although he was not an experienced diver and had never been below fifty feet before, he helped me on with the doubles and went down my lifeline to the bottom at 155 feet where I tried to decompress while Phil returned to the surface to get more tanks and divers.

While descending, at about 140 feet, the pains began to leave my body. I worked my way up slowly, but the damage had already been done by my forced rapid ascent.

As I ascended the pains came back again. I met Phil at about 130 feet, coming down to see how I was. Meanwhile, Shirley telephoned Tiny Wirs. Tiny set the wheels in motion by alerting the North Port Ambulance Squad and the Sarasota County Sheriff's Department. By the time I got back to the thirty-foot ledge I was met by Tiny and Dimitri Rebikoff, who took over decompressing me to the surface.

17

~~~~~~~~~~~~~~~~~~ *ordeal by air*

SHIRLEY CAN BEST relate what happened after I got to the surface:

While Tiny and Dimitri were decompressing Bill in the springs, Charlie Patton and Phil Levine were busy pumping up all available tanks and carrying them to the water's edge. The ambulance siren alerted the residents who lived near the springs, and soon a small crowd had gathered around anxiously awaiting Bill's emergence from the water, which finally occurred at 6 P.M.

Bill's first remark when he came out of the water was,

"What the hell is that ambulance doing here?" He began to stagger drunkenly out of the water and decided that he had to go back in to wash off the mud so he wouldn't get the ambulance dirty!

Tiny, realizing that Bill was unable to walk once he was out of the buoyant water, grabbed him under the arms. Tiny is a huge, powerful man who was once a professional football player for the Baltimore Colts. He brought him ashore. The ambulance attendants immediately began administering oxygen and hurried him into the ambulance.

While Bill was en route to the Venice Hospital Emergency Room, Patton contacted the Coast Guard station in St. Petersburg to determine the procedure for getting Bill to a recompression chamber should it be necessary.

When I arrived at Venice Hospital Bill was on a table receiving oxygen. He looked gray; his lips were an unhealthy shade of blue. The doctor in charge ordered a chest X ray to see if he had suffered an air embolism.

After examining the X rays they told me that I could take Bill home. I should have realized that the average doctor knows little about the bends and other decompression sicknesses, but I knew even less and took the doctor at his word. I asked a nurse to bring me a wheelchair since Bill was unable to stand or walk. I noted too that his speech was slurred.

After paying our bill I wheeled Bill out of the hospital with Rebikoff's help and drove home to our house in Nokomis. With more help I finally got him undressed and into bed.

As before, his skin was gray, his lips blue and his chest spotted with corpselike mottling, which is one of the symptoms of decompression sickness. I was alarmed at his appearance but tried to keep my concern from him. I called to Dimitri, who was washing off and packing up his diving and camera gear, preparing to leave for the airport to return to Melbourne. When he saw Bill's appearance he said, "Bill looks bad. We must fly him immediately to the nearest recompression chamber."

I tried to phone Charlie Patton, who had all the information about the location of the chamber from his earlier calls. Unable to reach him, I called Tiny Wirs, who arrived in minutes still dressed in his wet bathing suit, his dry clothes over his arm. He made the necessary phone call to the Coast Guard in St. Petersburg, advising them that Rebikoff's twin-engine Apache was available. They told him to load Bill into the plane and they would contact the plane by radio with further instructions. Dimitri was to fly as low as possible because the decrease in pressure could cause further damage to Bill.

We drove Tiny, Dimitri and Bill to the Venice Airport. The Sheriff's Department had phoned the airport earlier to ensure that the plane would be gassed up in case we needed it. Unfortunately the attendant really filled it up —wing tanks, tail tanks and all. Bill and Dimitri weighed over 200 pounds each and Tiny weighed over 300. With all that gas and all those big men, we had to remove every piece of extra equipment—cans of oil, cameras, etc.— before takeoff. The plane was rated to carry five passengers with an average weight of 150 pounds each. Tiny went along to assist Dimitri with Bill and the navigation, since in addition to his other talents Tiny is also a former Air Force pilot.

Flying at 800 feet or less, Dimitri flew along Alligator

Alley and stayed in constant touch by radio to avoid other planes that might be in the area. Advised by the Coast Guard, they flew to Fort Lauderdale-Hollywood International Airport, where they were met by the personnel of the Naval Ordinance Laboratory Test Facility, who transported Bill to the nearby recompression chamber. There he was started on Table 6 recompression schedule at 11:36 P.M.

While the divers were flying to Fort Lauderdale, Bill's son Willy, Phil Levine, Ada Rebikoff and I drove to Fort Lauderdale, arriving about 1:30 A.M. Dimitri and Tiny found motel units for us nearby, thanks to Chief Sanders at the Naval Ordinance Lab. It was spring vacation time in Fort Lauderdale and the college students had arrived en masse, leaving few rooms to be had. I stayed with Bill, observing him through portholes in the recompression chamber. His appearance was still frightful: gray skin and blue lips. The recompression chamber, a huge steel tank with valves and pipes and hissing air, looked to me, a Sunday-diving housewife, like a setting for a science-fiction horror movie.

Chief Sanders had contacted Dr. James A. Johnson, USN, at the submarine base in Key West and Dr. William H. Spar, USN, at the USN Experimental Diving Unit in Washington, D.C. With the collaboration of these two naval authorities on recompression procedure, Chief Sanders and his four-man crew—CWO Gladdings, EMC Brannin, GMCS Grund and ST-1 Gemma—worked through the night, monitoring the valves and gauges on the huge steel chamber.

Brannin was inside the chamber with Bill, urging him to "breathe deep," while the others spelled each other on the gauges, alternating compressed air and oxygen, following programmed instructions simulating a dive to sixty feet and subsequent ascent to the surface. The first recompression lasted until about 4:30 A.M. These men had either been on duty all day Saturday or had been enjoying their day off. Each of them had given up their free time to assist in bringing Bill back to the "world of the living." With plenty of Navy coffee and their salty conversation, we made it through the night and the lab lost some of its earlier horror-movie aspect for me.

Sanders was concerned that Bill wasn't getting sufficient oxygen through his mask. He believed that this was due to an improper seal between the mask and Bill's face. Bill's newly grown "Fu Manchu" moustache was causing a defective seal. While he should have been consuming about 500 pounds of oxygen per hour, he had only taken a total of 500 pounds in over five hours.

Inside the chamber Brannin was trying desperately to keep Bill awake and breathing deeply. But Brannin, who had been out on the beach all day, was having difficulty staying awake himself. Whenever the "Breathe deep, Bill" began to get faint, one of the men outside the chamber would rap with a big wrench on the steel tank and order, "Hey! Wake up in there!"

When the gauges indicated that Bill and Brannin had "reached the surface," it was time to remove them from the pressurized chamber. Bill had been lying on a Navy bunk constructed of steel pipes and canvas. As he sat up, with the assistance of several Navy men, the canvas ripped and down he went on the steel grid deck of the chamber, his rear on the deck, his feet and shoulders stuck fast in the canvas. After the tension of the night and preceding day, everyone broke up with laughter, including the patient. Prying him out of the slit in the canvas and pulling him through the hatch on the end of the chamber (a space about four feet in diameter) was like an Abbott and Costello comedy.

When he was finally extricated from the chamber, it was obvious that he still could not walk alone and that his skin still prickled. He would have to go back into the chamber again later in the day after some much needed sleep at the motel.

Bill is a big man and required the help of several strong men present to get him outside, down the steps and into our car. Sanders, in his car, led me to the motel and helped me get Bill out of the car and into bed. Willy and Phil had returned from taking Tiny to Miami to catch a plane back to Sarasota and they decided to sleep in the car, since it was already 5 A.M.

We caught a few hours sleep and awakened at 7 A.M. It was necessary for the Rebikoffs to leave for Melbourne, as they had reservations on a plane from Nassau for France that day. Willy, Phil, Ada, Dimitri and I drove to the airport and loaded their diving and camera equipment from the car to their plane. Then Willy and I drove back to the motel. Not only were Bill's legs paralyzed, but he had no feeling in his left arm and very little in his right. To be so helpless was depressing for Bill, who had always been the stalwart in emergencies.

After breakfast Bill felt that he should go to the bathroom, as he'd not been since Saturday morning, twenty-four hours earlier. Willy had hitched a ride back to Venice and Bill and I were alone. I pulled Bill to his feet, but not being able to stand, he crashed to the floor, taking me down with him. Finally, I rolled him onto the two bath towels and dragged and pushed him across the floor into the tiny bathroom with the lavatory right in front of the shower.

Deciding that it was simpler to get him into the shower than up onto the toilet, I crammed him into the shower stall, using my feet to push and bracing myself against the opposite wall. Then I turned on the water and handed him a bar of soap.

Since the only clothes I had with me were borrowed from a good friend at Warm Mineral Springs when I left there to go to the hospital on Saturday, and I didn't want to get them wet, I decided to strip for action, in order to get Bill out of the shower. That was another Abbott and Costello comedy! Imagine two adults slithering around the floor in the tiny shower, water all over everything and Bill so soap-slippery that I couldn't get a grip on him. He had to shave off his moustache before the next session in the chamber, but trying to shave sitting in a shower with no control over one's hands is quite a feat! I offered to help him, but he insisted that he could at least shave himself. I was afraid he'd miss and shave off his nose.

Once the ordeal of shaving was over, I turned on the water again to rinse him off, but it was impossible to drag him out of the shower until he was dry. It had been raining outdoors, and without air conditioning the humidity was as bad inside the bathroom as it was outside.

When Bill was dry enough to grip, I dragged him out of the shower feet-first. Once again I rolled him onto the towels, dripping wet by this time, and slid him across the floor. With a huge effort of pulling, pushing, lifting and rolling, I finally got him back into bed. At this point, exhausted and hurting from a shoulder sprained the previous week, I was just about at the end of my endurance.

At 2 P.M. the indefatigable Chief Sanders arrived at the motel to help me load Bill into the car and take him back to the Ordinance Depot, where we went for his second and final session in the chamber. All of the men who had been on duty the previous night were on hand to begin once more the long ascent from the bottom.

Since the bunk had broken the night before it was necessary to put Bill directly on the steel grid deck of the chamber, protected by a folded blanket. Fortunately he didn't have much feeling in his lower back and legs. More of the good-natured kidding, more Navy coffee, and at 8:30 Sunday night Bill was brought out of the recompression chamber.

He still couldn't walk. The Navy authorities felt it was imperative for Bill to go immediately to a hospital where neurologists could assess the damage done to his nervous system. I knew that with Bill's small pension from the Air Force we could never afford to pay the bill in a civilian hospital. So we loaded him into the car and I drove back to the motel and packed. Then we drove directly to Homestead Air Force Hospital, sixty miles south, only to find no neurologist on the staff.

Dr. Bernard Waltuck, medical officer on duty, assisted by Staff Sgt. Allison, Sgt. Brister and Airmen First Class Daimbra and Passanisi, did everything possible to make Bill comfortable. A catheter was inserted to relieve his acute bladder discomfort.

Dr. Waltuck meanwhile contacted the two Navy recompression authorities in Washington and Key West. On their advice he decided to move Bill to a hospital where he could begin treatment to remove the nitrogen bubbles lodged in his spine, causing paralysis of his arms and the lower part of his body. Dr. Waltuck telephoned the Veterans Hospital and the Jackson Memorial Hospital in Miami. This was about 1 A.M. Monday morning, and the difficulties of getting in touch with a neurologist in the middle of the night on a weekend were eventually overcome. Dr. Waltuck told an airman to take Bill by ambulance to Miami and he would instruct him by radio which hospital could handle the case. I was too exhausted by this time to drive to Miami and find a hotel room, so I spent the night in the Visiting Officers' Quarters on the base and drove to Miami the following morning.

The choice was the Veterans Hospital, a fully staffed and beautifully equipped facility built only four years before. When I arrived at the hospital just before noon, Dr. Richard Sax had already examined Bill and begun his medication and treatment. I left Miami that afternoon to come home to our two boys, knowing that all that could possibly be done for Bill would be done by the excellent residents and staff at the VA Hospital.

On Friday our good friend Jim Smith, another diver, took a day off from his job at General Development Corporation in Port Charlotte to drive me to Miami for a visit. The improvement in Bill's condition was miraculous, thanks to Dr. Sax and his associates, Drs. John Kitchen and Mihai Dimanescu. Bill was up and about, trying to use a walker but waddling like a duck, not having regained complete control of his feet.

Unfortunately I had to return home that day. But Bill's improvement since Sunday night was so great that I didn't feel I was leaving him hopelessly paralyzed. Each day he telephoned me from a port-a-phone wheeled into his room by members of the volunteer staff.

Finally, on March 31, thirteen days after the accident, I was able to bring Bill home. The worst of the ordeal was over. Ahead lay many months of painful but gradual recovery from the numbing paralysis in Bill's lower extremities. But thanks to his incredible determination to overcome the problem, his health finally returned almost as good as ever. No doubt too, one of the most important things that hastened this miracle was Bill's daily trips back to Warm Mineral Springs, where he hobbled to the water's edge on his crutches, donned his diving gear and swam back down into his beloved springs.

18

in pursuit of ice age man

WHEN I RETURNED to dive at Warm Mineral Springs I was still suffering some paralysis from the waist down, but I felt that continuous diving with proper precaution was one of the most therapeutic things I could do to correct the problem. And it eventually did. During this time I met an excellent diver, Les Koher, who owned his own dive shop in Indiana and now lived in Nokomis, Florida. Les was a first-class diver, the only person I have ever trusted to dive back inside the deep tunnel without worrying me too much. Les dived with me whenever he could get away on weekends, and was a big help in maintaining our diving equipment.

It was interesting to me that periodically I noticed large rib bones embedded in the limestone, sometimes huge clusters of them. Seeing them made me believe that early man drove huge prehistoric creatures into the spring and then dragged or floated them to a ledge to butcher them for food. Since some areas of the underwater cavern have nearly vertical walls, this led Dr. Goggin to remark once, "If Early Man inhabited Warm Mineral Springs, he must have been quite an Alpinist. . . ."

This need not have been so. Modern Florida has abundant vines twenty to thirty feet long, and it wouldn't have taken too much intelligence for Early Man to fashion himself a vine rope ladder enabling him to climb up and down the walls of the spring. I found evidence at the sixty-foot depth that suggested Early Man may have drilled holes in the rock walls and inserted wood pegs in them. In one place in the springs there is still a wooden peg in such a hole. Clausen found similarly shaped pegs in the walls of Little Salt Spring during his archaeological investigation. They carbon date between 9,325 and 9,-965 years old. Whether or not these pegs supported vine ladders is still a matter of conjecture. But Early Man drove them into the wall of the spring for some purpose.

One day I found an unusual piece of material in the springs that had a bright metallic coating similar to tarnished silver or pewter. I brought up a piece and gave it to Dottie Davis of the Sarasota Historical Commission. She in turn passed it on to a local geologist, who analyzed it and said it was pentlandite, an alloy of iron sulfide and nickel. In past years when I was more actively excavating and removing sediments from the rocks I had found large quantities of this material coating some of the rock cliff. Lord knows what would have happened to archaeological exploration in the springs if this material had proved to be silver. Imagine an underwater silver mine! Apparently, however, this pentlandite formed wherever fresh water leached through fissures in the rocks from the surface, causing a precipitation of the minerals on the rocks.

On another dive I saw a large piece of black rocklike material that penetrated deep into the Miocene bedrock. Could it possibly be a meteorite, I wondered? I sawed off a piece of the black rock and sent it to the Smithsonian Institution in Washington, D.C., for analysis. They reported that it could not possibly be a meteorite because it lacked nickel, and all meteorites contained nickel. After receiving this information I read up on the subject and found that many meteorites contain no nickel. When I had a similar piece of the material analyzed in Texas, it was found to be a chondrite meteorite. So far as I know, this is the first one to be removed from sedimentary material.

One of the strangest discoveries in the springs was large deposits of vegetation, mostly fernlike material embedded in the stalactites. Often the vegetation was completely replaced by the highly concentrated lime water dripping from the stalactites, leaving a beautiful calcified leaf. Apparently the vegetation was growing on the stalactites when they were forming above sea level, which would mean that these delicate, encrusted ferns in their brittle limestone cases were probably well over 10,000 years old. When I brought up a piece of this uniquely calcified vegetation and broke it open, I would find the fern still sealed inside the mineral deposit. As soon as it was exposed to air, it disappeared. The same occurs with wood items found in the spring and undoubtedly of great age. The highly mineralized spring water preserves the wood perfectly until it is exposed to air, then it shrinks and rapidly deteriorates.

In October 1972 I was invited to join an expedition headed out into the Gulf of Mexico in an effort to find what was called "Mud Boil Spring." Accompanying us on this trip was hydrologist Fran Kohout and his wife Layne, Shirley Royal, Dottie Davis, Bill Mote of the Mote Marine Laboratory, George Wheeler III, and Wilburn "Sonny" Cockrell, our new state marine archaeologist.

We were on the fifty-four-foot yacht *Great White,* research vessel of philanthropist Bill Mote.

As we approached the spring about twelve miles offshore from Fort Myers Beach we could see the difference in the water color, which looked like an oil slick on the surface. We later found that this was caused by hot, highly mineralized saltwater gushing from the depths of the earth, diffusing its minerals in the much colder Gulf waters.

Anchoring the vessel over it, the divers went down to see this unique phenomenon, following the anchor line to a depth of sixty-five feet, where hot water surged out of a four-foot long, eight-inch-wide rock crevice, the main source of the spring. Apparently the temperature of the spring was attractive to fish because many circled around the area and seemed to bathe in its warmth. Fran Kohout took numerous water samples at its source and found that the water temperature where it emerged from the crevice was 97° F.—more evidence for his theory about geothermal pressure from the Boulder Zone.

We spent two days at the Mud Boil Spring, photographing and taking samples. The trip gave us an excellent opportunity to meet Sonny Cockrell, who had taken over the job of state archaeologist when Clausen left. I told Cockrell about Warm Mineral Springs and described the human mandible I had found. I said, "If you ever come to Warm Mineral Springs and excavate, you will find things that will make both you and the springs world famous."

I'm sure Sonny took this with a grain of salt. Still, as usual, I left the invitation open for him to come and evaluate the site for himself.

A month later Cockrell found an opportunity to accept the invitation. I dove with him and took him on a tour of the springs, pointing out various bones that I had found in the sediments but left untouched. When he saw the lower human mandible in place, which I had discovered over a year before, he was quite excited. He cleared out some of the sediments surrounding it and was able to squeeze into the small crevice where it was. With careful excavating around the jawbone, Cockrell uncovered the skull from which the mandible had come, and other parts of the skeleton. Diving with Sonny during this exciting week were Larry Workman, Dennis English and Tommy Gore from the state, and Marion Almy and Dottie Davis from the Sarasota County Historical Commission.

In order to fully evaluate the skull, Cockrell wanted to have the geology of the site properly identified and recorded. He contacted Dr. Vance Haynes of Southern Methodist University in Texas and asked for his assistance. Dr. Haynes, a leading authority on the relationship of Pleistocene megafauna and man, joined the team. Diving with Cockrell, he determined that it was definitely an archaeologically important site, worthy of further effort. After that, it was necessary for the State of Florida to appropriate sufficient funds for a full-scale operation backed by a team of scientists to oversee various phases of the underwater dig.

Once again when it appeared that qualified authorities were finally going to see what we had been saving for them for so long, I continued establishing underwater guidelines to the most important features so there would be no wasted efforts.

Frequently this was a group undertaking involving a number of divers: Les Koher, Marion Almy, Dottie Davis and my wife. Dottie's husband, Ralph "Bud" Davis, gave us a beautiful brass compass rose which we set at the exact center of the springs, sixty-five feet below the surface. With the compass rose in place we secured lines going to all the major points of the compass, and one going straight down to the debris cone on the bottom. This compass and line system created something of a deepwater spiderweb of lines leading to all the important finds I had made to date. Marion Almy, who was working on her Master of Arts Degree in Public Archaeology, recorded them all on a chart so that when the scientific team of divers arrived they would be able to go directly down to any point in the springs.

The following January Sonny Cockrell came back with a small work crew and Dr. Reynold Ruppé, chairman of the Anthropology Department at Arizona State University. Dr. Ruppé, one of the foremost authorities on

Paleo-Indians in North America, had been Cockrell's professor during his undergraduate days at Arizona State.

After a thorough examination of the site before beginning the excavation, it was determined that it would be necessary to remove several huge boulders and stalagmites that covered the area to be excavated.

Helping in this effort in addition to the regular crew was George Wheeler III, grandson of Fred Daley who had financed my exploration in Warm Mineral Springs for the past three years. On his first day working on the project, George found a large Megalodon shark tooth embedded in the Miocene bedrock close to the site. There was no indication that the tooth had been used as a tool; therefore it was left untouched, firmly cemented in place as it had been for many millions of years.

To remove large boulders and stalagmites, we improvised a barrel lift system capable of lifting these great rocks weighing over 4,000 pounds apiece, a total of 3 1/2 tons of overlaying boulders. The method we devised was similar to the one we had used to raise the stalactites previously. Fifty-five-gallon drums were submerged and chained to the boulders in clusters. Air was injected into the drums and, as they began to lift, guidelines eased them out and away from the immediate area for deposit elsewhere in the springs.

After the large boulders were removed and the underlying sediments cleared, we were ready for the big day: February 5, 1973. With a host of visiting dignitaries on hand and the event covered by all the major newspapers and television services, Cockrell and Dr. Ruppé recovered the skull from the site forty-five feet underwater.

The fact that this human skeletal material lay beneath broken stalagmites and stalactites indicated that it may have been a human burial site. Later carbon-14 dating made from organic material found there returned a date of 10,300 years B.P. (Before the Present). This was an average of twenty radiocarbon dates made on samples removed from the immediate area. The find was judged to be the oldest verified human remains recovered from a burial site in the southeastern United States.

After this major recovery the excavation was closed and sealed by the archaeologists. Several months later Cockrell, assisted by Marion Almy, returned to secure fossil pollen samples in and around the burial site for carbon-14 dating. While collecting the samples he uncovered a remarkably fine atlatl or spear-throwing device used by Early Man. It was made of shell, carved with a hook on one end for engaging the shaft of a short spear. What appeared to be pine pitch resin adhesive was still on the artifact. This, along with bindings, apparently secured it to the end of a short-handled launching stick.

Cockrell felt that this artifact was of greater significance than the skull he had found several months earlier. Actually, the atlatl hook found in conjunction with the skull and other human remains increased their significance, particularly when one realizes that this burial and accompanying artifact date back long before the use of bows and arrows, before the First Dynasty of the Egyptian Pharaohs, and 8,000 years before the birth of Christ!

The following January I began constructing a new house at Warm Mineral Springs. Although I'd built hundreds of houses in the past, working as a general contractor, I decided that this one was to be different. Shirley and I searched until we found plans for a round house. Together we cleared the lot, which was covered with thick vines and heavy palmetto growth. Sometimes we had the help of friends, but for the most part we did it alone. Part of the day I would spend diving in Warm Mineral Springs and part I would spend working on the house, digging the footing and laying the blocks. What eventually became the focal point of the entire home is a round fronted fireplace faced entirely with sawed sections of stalactites and stalagmites that I hauled up from the bottom of the springs, interspersed with sectioned pieces of fossil whale vertebra, mammoth teeth, mammoth tusk, agatized fossil coral, huge Megalodon shark teeth, heads of femurs from prehistoric mammoths and an assortment of other fossils that came almost entirely from the unique four-fathom boneyard off Venice Beach. To say the least, our "prehistoric" fireplace is quite a conversation piece.

Much to my surprise, on February 14, 1974, I was honored at an awards breakfast in Sarasota at which Secretary of State Richard "Dick" Stone presented me with a plaque from the State of Florida. It read: "In grateful appreciation to Colonel William Royal for his contribution to our understanding of man's past and future through his discovery and subsequent preservation of Early Man remains at Warm Mineral Springs."

At the occasion Secretary Stone commended underwater archaeologist Sonny Cockrell, State Representative Robert Johnson, State Senator Warren Henderson, Mote Marine Laboratory President William Mote, the Sarasota County Historical Commission and members of the Fred Daley family, without whose support the project at Warm Mineral Springs would never have been possible.

Although I am basically a shy man, I must admit I was deeply moved by the award. To finally receive recognition after all the years I had been ridiculed for my ideas and the things we had found in the springs was most gratifying.

Apparently the newspapers mentioned it fairly widely because I received calls from friends all over the country who read about it. One of the headlines from the *Washington Star-News* was especially amusing: DIVERS FIND PROVEN NO SKULDUGGERY. In light of what we had gone through in the past trying to prove the authenticity of the skull with the brain in it, this headline seemed particularly apt.

What started so many years ago with my discovery of underwater stalactites, and all that followed, was finally achieving fruition. And in subsequent years it continued. The knowledge compounded itself from a small step forward in modern times to become a giant stride backward into our ancient past.

And this, apparently, is still just the beginning. A few years after the major find at Warm Mineral Springs, underwater archaeologist Carl Clausen, who had earlier sampled what both of these springs had to offer archaeologically, returned to Little Salt Spring under a special grant from the General Development Foundation and continues to make increasingly important finds from the depths of the spring. Most recently on a ledge ninety feet below the surface the remains of a giant prehistoric land tortoise was found impaled on two shaped wooden stakes that carbon date to 13,500 years B.P. (Before the

Present). Also found in shallower depths was part of a shaped wood hunting boomerang, the first of its kind ever found associated with Early Man in the Western Hemisphere.

Through the efforts of State Representative Robert Johnson, the State of Florida appropriated almost $100,-000 to launch a thorough archaeological investigation of Warm Mineral Springs by Cockrell and his team to uncover and record more of its unique archaeological history. Even the remarkable underwater prehistoric topography off Venice Beach was not overlooked. Dr. Reynold Ruppé returned with a grant to explore and chart the ancient submerged riverbeds in search of Early Man sites along their banks—an ongoing project that one day may lead us into the depths of the ocean and to the very brink of the Continental Shelf to find the oldest roots of our ancient past.

Scientific acceptance of what I found in the springs had taken seventeen years. Hopefully our progress in the future will move more swiftly. Now that we're all in step and finally moving in the right direction, all I ask is the chance to play a small part in the coming big adventure, the next chapter in our search for Ice Age Man.

This is not the end of the story, it is simply,

To be continued . . .

index

Printed in the United States
4869

9 780595 003891